On Mystery, Ineffability, Silence and Musical Symbolism

READING AUGUSTINE

Series Editor:
Miles Hollingworth

Reading Augustine presents books that offer personal, nuanced and oftentimes literary readings of Saint Augustine of Hippo. Each time, the idea is to treat Augustine as a spiritual and intellectual icon of the Western tradition, and to read through him to some or other pressing concern of our current day. Or to some enduring issue or theme. In this way, the writers follow the model of Augustine himself, who produced his famous output of words and ideas in active tussle with the world in which he lived. When the series launched, this approach could raise eyebrows, but now that technology and pandemics have brought us into the world and society like never before, and when scholarship is expected to live the same way and responsibly, the series is well-set and thriving.

Volumes in the series:
On Music, Sense, Affect, and Voice, Carol Harrison
On Solitude, Conscience, Love and Our Inner, and Outer Lives, Ron Haflidson
On Creation, Science, Disenchantment, and the Contours of Being and Knowing, Matthew W. Knotts
On Agamben, Arendt, Christianity, and the Dark Arts of Civilization, Peter Iver Kaufman
On Self-Harm, Narcissism, Atonement, and the Vulnerable Christ, David Vincent Meconi
On Faith, Works, Eternity, and the Creatures We Are, André Barbera
On Time, Change, History, and Conversion, Sean Hannan
On Compassion, Healing, Suffering, and the Purpose of the Emotional Life, Susan Wessel

On Consumer Culture, Identity, the Church and the Rhetorics of Delight, Mark Clavier
On Creativity, Liberty, Love and the Beauty of the Law, Todd Breyfogle
On Education, Formation, Citizenship and the Lost Purpose of Learning, Joseph Clair
On Ethics, Politics and Psychology in the Twenty-First Century, John Rist
On God, The Soul, Evil and the Rise of Christianity, John Peter Kenney
On Love, Confession, Surrender and the Moral Self, Ian Clausen
On Memory, Marriage, Tears, and Meditation, Margaret R. Miles

On Mystery, Ineffability, Silence and Musical Symbolism

Laurence Wuidar

BLOOMSBURY ACADEMIC
LONDON • NEW YORK • OXFORD • NEW DELHI • SYDNEY

BLOOMSBURY ACADEMIC
Bloomsbury Publishing Plc
50 Bedford Square, London, WC1B 3DP, UK
1385 Broadway, New York, NY 10018, USA
29 Earlsfort Terrace, Dublin 2, Ireland

BLOOMSBURY, BLOOMSBURY ACADEMIC and the Diana logo are trademarks of
Bloomsbury Publishing Plc

First published in Great Britain 2021

Copyright © Laurence Wuidar, 2021

Laurence Wuidar has asserted her right under the Copyright,
Designs and Patents Act, 1988, to be identified as Author of this work.

Cover image: Naples, Spanish quarter, 2013 © Laurence Wuidar

All rights reserved. No part of this publication may be reproduced or
transmitted in any form or by any means, electronic or mechanical,
including photocopying, recording, or any information storage or
retrieval system, without prior permission in writing from the publishers.

Bloomsbury Publishing Inc does not have any control over, or responsibility
for, any third-party websites referred to or in this book. All internet addresses given in
this book were correct at the time of going to press. The author and publisher regret any
inconvenience caused if addresses have changed or sites have ceased to exist, but can
accept no responsibility for any such changes.

A catalogue record for this book is available from the British Library.

Library of Congress Cataloging-in-Publication Data
Names: Wuidar, Laurence, 1978- author.
Title: On mystery, ineffability, silence, and musical symbolism / Laurence Wuidar.
Other titles: Simbologia musicale nei commenti ai Salmi di Agostino. English
Description: New York : Bloomsbury Academic, 2021. | Series: Reading Augustine |
"This book was originally published in 2014 by Mimesis Edizioni, Milan, as La simbologia
musicale nei commenti ai Salmi di Agostino"–Translator's note. | Includes bibliographical
references and index. |
Identifiers: LCCN 2021011809 (print) | LCCN 2021011810 (ebook) |
ISBN 9781350228788 (paperback) | ISBN 9781350228795 (hardback) |
ISBN 9781350228801 (epub) | ISBN 9781350228818 (pdf)
Subjects: LCSH: Music–Religious aspects–Christianity. | Augustine,
of Hippo, Saint, 354–430–Knowledge–Music. | Augustine, of Hippo,
Saint, 354–430–Criticism and interpretation.
Classification: LCC ML3921.2 .W8513 2021 (print) | LCC ML3921.2 (ebook) |
DDC 261.5/78–dc23
LC record available at https://lccn.loc.gov/2021011809
LC ebook record available at https://lccn.loc.gov/2021011810

ISBN:	HB:	978-1-3502-2879-5
	PB:	978-1-3502-2878-8
	ePDF:	978-1-3502-2881-8
	ePUB:	978-1-3502-2880-1

Series: Reading Augustine

Typeset by Integra Software Services Pvt. Ltd.

To find out more about our authors and books visit www.bloomsbury.com
and sign up for our newsletters.

CONTENTS

Translator's Note viii
Preface, by Paolo Gozza x
Premiss xiii
Abbreviations xxi

Introduction, or first steps in to the text(s) 1

1   The Christian 31

2   The Prophet and the Saint 65

3   Christ 77

4   The Father 109

Notes 131
Bibliography 154
Index 164

TRANSLATOR'S NOTE

This book was originally published in 2014 by Mimesis Edizioni, Milan, as *La simbologia musicale nei commenti ai Salmi di Agostino*. I am very grateful to Mimesis Edizioni, and particularly to Pamela Lainati, their Foreign Rights Manager, for being so gracious in gifting us the English language rights to make this translation.

Likewise, Laurence would like to give special thanks to Nicoletta Guidobaldi, Academic Director of the series at Mimesis Edizioni in which her book originally appeared. This series is *Le immagini della Musica*. Laurence would like to thank Nicoletta for her courage and imagination in taking on Laurence's book, and for her clever idea to include an Introduction with a Bibliography in order to make the book seem more acceptable to academic eyes.

Laurence Wuidar's career certainly has taken its own path and this book which is pioneering even by Continental standards has gained significant notice for its method as much as for its results. See, for example, the long and admiring response to it from Professor Vittorino Grossi of the Pontifical Patristics Academy, The Augustinianum, Rome, published as 'L'immagine musicale nelle Enarrationes in Psalmos di Agostino: L'interazione con la teologia "affetttiva"', *Augustinianum* Vol. 56, Issue 1, June 2016, 207–33.

For my part, I have included in this translation some thoughts of my own that occurred along the way. They are clearly set apart in square brackets and are there for what they are worth. They are not necessary, so ignore them if you prefer. Otherwise, they fill in some of the gaps left by Laurence's method (or better, perhaps, her technique) in the nature of its case. What Laurence has noticed is that Augustine uses musical symbolism as a progressive and accumulating method of protection. Of protecting what? Well, it would seem the sacred and mysterious place in the interior of the human being into which God speaks, when he speaks. This place cannot be entered into, except by God. Thus, its contents are by definition beyond judgement, and must be protected from judgement. By her technique, Laurence tracks and arranges for us the progressive and cumulative aspect in Augustine's musical symbolism, from where it starts in a logically and historically determinate world depicted by airwaves and sound to where it ends, in the ecstatic silent music of our interior place in which God may ask us to do wild, even crazy things by the world's standards.

In this sense, I am extremely grateful to Paolo Gozza, Chair Emeritus of the Philosophy of Music at the University of Bologna, for contributing his Preface, in which he marks the points at which Laurence's technique then challenges and enriches the predominately historical study of music today. There is something to be gained by uncritically and unselfconsciously going on the trip with Augustine in this matter. Because at the end of it we do in fact encounter new and important knowledge. But first we have to get there.

Miles Hollingworth, Series Editor

PREFACE, BY PAOLO GOZZA

The subject of this book is musical symbolism as we find it in the writings of Saint Augustine of Hippo. But this will perhaps be the first time that this subject will have been pursed in this way, with Laurence Wuidar encountering the great Christian philosopher hand-to-hand, on the page, throwing herself into the melee of his musical imagery and treating it as metaphorical, both for theology and anthropology. What the results of this will illustrate is that there exists, and especially across texts less-frequented by students of Augustine, a veritable anthology of images rich in theological and anthropological-musical content; and all expressed in the musical key. The case in point will be Augustine's commentaries on the Psalms, in which the Word of God quite literally unites itself with the intonation of the liturgist, so that music and theology are seen to face each other and run with each other in the daily practice of the Christian and his song.

In the commentaries on the Psalms, and in the sermons and in the letters – and in a manner indeed more explicit than in his other writings on music, such as in *De musica* itself, certain passages in *Confessiones* and certain pages in *De Trinitate* and *De ordine* – Augustine constructs an extraordinary linguistic laboratory and a hermeneutics that turns the fundamental elements of music – viz., rhythm, tempo, listening, sound, voice, song, instrumentation – into the symbolic vehicles for expressing and explaining theological concepts – viz., the Divine Mind, the Word, Eternity, the Figure of Christ, the Cross, the Transfiguration, the Saints and the Prophets. In the course of this febrile exegetical exercise, music assumes the role of an exceptional and majestic relief, showing itself to be superior to all other discourses and reflections in its capacity to turn human knowledge to the mysteries of the Christian faith. There is, moreover, in Augustine (and it is Wuidar who shows it to us), a diffuse and active iconography in which the Christian comes to the threshold of the Divine thanks to the enhancement of their own musical imagery and their sense for it. In this hermeneutical context, musical images activate a fundamental transition: that is, they open the gateway to symbolic constructions, in which image and symbol work together in order to orientate the objects and forms of musical experience towards the world of theological truth while at the same time and vice-versa, theological concepts are seen to migrate, quite naturally, towards the musical experience of man in general as much as to the Christian.

The musicological reflections of Laurence Wuidar in this book therefore add something important to the current state of musical knowledge. This is because today, we can no longer say what is the nature, let alone the function of 'music's image'. We have lost touch with it. For example, obvious as it must seem, we have only recently learnt to return the sound, or the 'sound-content', to the images, or iconographies, of music. For too long and because of this, the musical image has lacked status and seriousness within the modern discipline of musicology. The truth is to say that the general mode, or pattern, of modern thought has found itself at a disadvantage before an image which is in the nature of its case, evanescent. This in turn is doubtless due to the schism between eye and ear which does characterize our present culture. This study of Wuidar's seeks precisely to interpret Augustine's musical thinking in light of the synergy between eye and ear that is otherwise compromised by our cultural incapacity to acknowledge that which in man is united.

Men have eyes and ears, and I want to say that if there were ever a moment in Western culture when a major writer made appeal to both equally, and at once, then that moment was Augustine! From out of Wuidar's pages, emerges the *pictorialism* of Augustine. All the places of the world are images, while the soul is the place in which all of these images of the world are contained. All the places of the world are images of God, and these images in the world manifest God and his mind because each is an example of creation and construction. As Augustine will put it in one prominent example, when the writings of Paul are heard or read, each 'paints in their own mind' an image of the face of the Saint. In this sense, there is no working distinction between visual memory and verbal memory: the letters are images, and the book is a picture. Even the sounds of the letters are images, and the words resound in the mind as sonorous images of objects painted by the voice.

For Augustine, then, the image is never an 'object', a visible or acoustic fact of which one might take possession. The image is rather a pathway – it is a sensible and spiritual journey taken by the body and the mind together. Again, we might say that Augustine's musical reflections take us along a route through sonorous images, with these images always signposting and lighting the way back to God. This makes it that for Augustine, Man (the Christian) is himself a musical instrument; and the Prophet and the Saint then more so again. God is the supreme 'Music', and the Son of God has a musical nature, human and divine. The world, meanwhile, is an immense symphonic poem. Furthermore, the human mind becomes to a degree like unto the Divine Mind insofar as it can take and transform the flight of time into an image that resides outside of time – we are talking of the image of 'eternity'. Finally, the musical instruments actually constructed by man bear within themselves a musical intention that suggests the metaphorical and symbolical use to which they shall be put. That is to say, by constructing them in order to make music with them, man admits to the fact that only music shall illuminate for him the profoundest theological truths.

Created by God in his image, man moves amongst images and the Truth does not belong to him. If instead he were to possess the Truth, he would not be man but God. This applies especially to the man of learning and culture. The objects of knowledge are images, shadows, copies which defer ultimately to a reality of intimacy and depth that lies beyond human understanding. Likewise, the musical scores here on earth are but fleeting images of the immense score of Creation, great work of God's music. In Augustine, music's image is the bridge thrown between the sensible and spiritual life. More than any other, it leads the human mind up to the invisible and ineffable: all the way to the very silencing of history. However, this does not mean that music possesses a special nature, different to other earthly realities. All things on earth have the capacity to point beyond themselves in image and symbolism, to higher, otherworldly realities. If there is something special about music in this regard, it is that from the moment it leaves the strings, it is already image and symbol. Image and symbolism are its natural currency in the human it inspires and affects and it is for image and symbolism that it is loved and pursued therefore, and in the first place. When it comes to God, music may be our most natural highway to correct communion with Him.

PREMISS

It was just an idea. The idea to immerse myself in the writings of Augustine, come what may. To immerse myself in order to seek out and be affected by fragments that, if only they might be brought together in some special arrangement would – then – 'recompose' the human musical being – the 'musical man' – as Augustine saw him. From this deep-immersion reading within the texts, from primary material and from historical material, the mosaic that I was after would compose itself. This is what I believed. That is, I believed that from fragments set and articulated one to the other, and thereby inspiring each other and speaking to each other, might arise questions that in turn then would give strength to and revive before us the 'Augustinian imagination'. But specifically, the Augustinian imagination as it worked with and upon the images, metaphors, allegories and symbols of music. And more again, as it focused itself upon the figure central to all of this: Man as made in the *musical* image of the Word.[1]

What has never been in question is that to read Augustine on music is to come on to themes that after him would go on to be discussed for centuries within the theory of music in Europe. Augustine would delineate some of the themes fundamental to the musical culture of Western Christianity up to the late Renaissance. In the one part, this would be because he inherited accurately and with intelligence the questions on music already posed in the philosophies of ancient Greece; in the other part, because he ran into and formulated new problems and questions of his own. Altogether, he would lay the foundations for a way of thinking about music that would be part and parcel of his famous Christianizing of Platonic thought. In the history of European culture, music is an integral part of philosophical and theological thought. Not only because it constitutes one of the recognized steps in the science of the Divine, but because from the biblical sources themselves spring various musical problems pertaining to both man and God. Sacred

Scripture has been the font of a multiplicity of reflections that have enriched musical culture. These reflections are as much a part of the history of music as they are of the history of philosophy and of theology.

At this point I want to stress that it is for the reader who desires some historiographical references and some bibliographic information that I have added this Premiss. Likewise, the Introduction which follows it offers the intellectual background and the guide (if there can be such thing) to the experiment ahead of it. Otherwise, everything that is to follow takes place within the Augustinian texts themselves. This is what I meant by 'reviving' the Augustinian imagination in relation to music. Or what is the same thing (so far as I am concerned), of using music to smoke it into life. For the imagination of anyone let alone a genius like Augustine is a creative force that will therefore always elude and escape us if we focus only on the words it uses. I mean this. If we focus on the words and their meanings, then we fall into the traditional way of Western, scientific knowledge; in which in this case, Augustine would figure as an historical contributor to the established discipline of musicology. This discipline and its themes would come first, and Augustine's writings would come second. I am not saying that this way is wrong. I am just saying that, here is another way – and that I dreamed it up and followed it! And that I followed it because I am fascinated by Augustine's imagination and by how and why that imagination arranged the words as it did; and then by how and why that imagination saw its correspondent in the Divine imagination and in the arrangements of words that the Divine imagination made in the Scriptures. And if one is prepared to see it like this, and to go this far with it (as I did!), then of course one is dealing with a phenomenon that is musical rather than (logically) determinate and (logically) derivative.

> [*Editor:* You see, it really is the case that in a writer of imagination, the words go together as do the notes go together in music. And that if the effect on us the reader then is beautiful and moving, we are faced with something that really is a mystery. Because what makes it that a certain note should follow a certain other note other than the creative force of the imagination behind them, plus that imagination's determination to go after something true and beautiful (and therefore true

because beautiful)? And the same for words. And what makes it that we the listener or the reader can feel and enjoy the truth and the beauty except for our own imagination which can take its pleasure vicariously, in the example of how the notes or words were arranged originally, by their composer? At this point, we notice again the either/or with which we are playing. Either we can approach Augustine through the traditional methods of modern musicology or we can approach him in Laurence's way, 'corpo a corpo' as she put it in the original Italian of this book, in which truth and beauty are determined not by empirical knowledge but by something that defies such stability of meaning and which therefore we are bound to call 'supernatural'. In this place, the Divine imagination and Augustine's imagination and our imagination appreciate each other until that sheer appreciation becomes what is true and beautiful. And how different that is to formulas of words that must mean the same one thing to everyone equally, in order to be doctrine; or knowledge. On this disturbing point, we reach the acme of Augustine's ambition as a writer, stated by him many times, but most famously at *Confessiones* XII, 31, 42:

Surely I myself – and I speak this fearlessly from my heart – if I were to write anything for the summit of authority, I would prefer to write in such manner that my words would sound forth the portion of truth each one man could take from these writings, rather than to put down one true thought so obviously that it would exclude all others.

This ambition to break the spell of words qua words and to use them instead like the notes in music, so that an unspoken truth and beauty may sound what it will to each in turn, and mysteriously, goes to the very heart of Augustine's mission as *Defensor fidei* and leaves him in a special position in letters and in the Church. It has been responsible for such euphemisms as that he was an 'unsystematic' thinker by the standards of his day, or even a 'postmodern' thinker by the standards of ours. What can be said better, perhaps, is that always and ultimately, the place he sought to defend was one into which only a living, musical Word could speak:

You are good and all-powerful, caring for each one of us as though the only one in Your care, and yet for all as for each individual.²

But now, back to some historiography and bibliography.]

Augustine appears in every history of music worthy of the name. Just as soon as the Ambrosian chant is reached, there you shall find alongside the name of Ambrose of Milan the name of his disciple, the future bishop of Hippo, and in particular, the testimonies of the latter concerning the chant of the Milanese Church – and especially his impressions as to its obscurity. These testimonies have been a 'blessed bread' to medieval historians. While to musicologists, Augustine has for this reason been the authority par excellence when it comes to representing and describing psalmody at the end of the fourth century. Even if the terms he uses can on occasion be unclear to a contemporary reader, within the universe of the medieval world, they stand as lights that illuminate this part of its history.³

What can still surprise many today from a more general point of view is that a father of the Church could be so interested in music as to have written an entire treatise on it – his *De musica* – originally to have been part of a much larger, encyclopaedic project of his on the liberal sciences, but which never saw the light of day.⁴ Professional musicologists, of course, know better, and studies by them on Augustine fairly abound.⁵ Historians of theology and philosophy with a special interest in music have also paid attention to him down the years and consistently.⁶ While in the field of aesthetics, *De musica* is cited often and with good effect. The musical concepts there developed by Augustine can be found featuring in debates on universal harmony as well as escaping from such strictly musicological circles to take part in much wider discussions on cosmic and artistic beauty.⁷ Otherwise, musicology tends to focus somewhat inevitably on the philological-historical side⁸ and on the technical aspects of metre, on rhythm and number. The study of Augustine's theory of rhythm – for some time now the most developed of the studies made of his understanding of music – together, of course, with the studies made of his distinction between intelligible and sensible number,⁹ themselves unfold within approaches and arcs which might be deemed (variously) philosophical, aesthetical, ethical, metaphysical or psychological.¹⁰

Notable studies also have been made of Augustine's Greek inheritance in this matter[11] and the general reception of Augustinian musical theory, such as the importance it has had in the history of musical aesthetics.[12]

Historians of the philosophy of music have especially been drawn in to Augustine via the question of time, which is a theme of central importance in his thought. For example, if you want to study the definition of 'silence' or the questions surrounding rhythm, then you will quickly discover that both are intimately connected to the question of time in Augustine. That is to say, on the one hand, to his treatments of eternity and the creation of the universe and then on the other hand, to his treatments of the will, the memory and reason.[13] In particular, if we consider how the proverbial *tempus fugit* finds its greatest human expressions and experiments in what we might call the 'arts of time' – viz., poetry, music and dance – then we will by reverse realize how and why music can be seen to permeate Augustine's most intimate interrogations of the vanishing instant, of the present, the past and the future. By the same token, music must surely be considered one of our – if not *the* – greatest sensible testimonies to the order of the universe, and therefore the Augustinian criteria of harmony and of beauty have gone on for that reason, and on that basis, to take an important place in the researches of historians of musical aesthetics.[14] And yet for all of this usefulness and appropriation, for all of these contributions that Augustine can be made to make to *our* disciplines, and to *our* understanding, his *De musica* remains as personal and as wilful as all his other writings. Its final, speculative book, replete with direct and indirect references to the Psalms and to the story of God incarnate demands from the reader a mind ready to voyage with him deep into philosophical and theological anthropology and into the meaning of music as humanly made, and Divinely inspired.

So be it for the typical panorama of research on our subject. I want now to mention briefly the work of Henri-Irénée Marrou, and to set it apart from the rest. For it does indeed stand out and needs to stand out still, in my opinion. His *Tristesse de l'historien*,[15] although dated in many respects, remains blazingly relevant in its invitation to history to question its methods and motives. By this is not meant the throwing open of history and historians to interdisciplinarity, which has largely taken place already anyway in the half decade and more since Marrou wrote. But rather a warning as to the tendency of the historical account to generate and follow out its own logic, once enough material and evidence have been accumulated. This is to say that history tends towards a single, 'true' version of events: which in turn is true because it can be the same one unambiguous thing to a (potential) infinity of human observers, or readers. By that stage, there is in fact very little for the historian to do, or be. He can only add a little bit here, or a little bit there. He has lost all scope for creativity and has become a slave to history's machine. Well, I want to say that it shouldn't surprise us that a student of Augustine should have written such a warning! Because it was Augustine himself who best and first invited us to revel in the possibilities of our creativity, both as writers and readers. And for his part, Marrou attempted to teach this lesson to modern hermeneutics. What is true is that you see something one way, and I see it another. This is the normal, natural way of humanity. Words and language make it appear as though the truth should lie in a single meaning, which we both attempt to put on. Not by chance, then, Marrou went on to write an essay on Augustine's *De musica*, in which he used its example to argue for a new path of research with respect to historical data and at the same time, orientated towards new horizons of meaning.

Beyond their obvious interest in his *De musica*, musicologists also give special attention to Augustine's *Confessiones*. This is for two reasons, or on two themes. The first is 'time', whose importance we have already signalled. While the second is 'sin'. Book XI of the *Confessiones* contains Augustine famous and full 'philosophy of time and eternity', into which he incorporates musical examples and preoccupations familiar from his earlier *De musica*. While Book X contains his equally famous reflections and remarks on pleasure, triggered by his memory of his first hearing the Church music in Milan.[16] If, ultimately, Augustine was able to confirm the utility and value of music at the heart of the liberal arts curriculum à la *De musica*, *Confessiones* X would show him to have remained equivocal on the value of music in church. This was due to his lasting impression of how music in that context can dominate its hearer by its sheer appeal of beauty, and as it were, lead them where it will by emotive and affective pull; in other words, beyond what its purely sacramental purpose should have been. It can then precipitate a man into sin by stoking the sensual side of his being. In saying this, Augustine was thinking of himself, and how he fell in this way on more than one occasion. In his opinion, only grace could save us from the 'runaway train' of this experience (the celebrated passage on this occurs at *Confessiones*, X, 33, 49–50).

Finally, in addition to *De musica* and *Confessiones*, the attention of researchers has focused itself on the *Enarrationes in Psalmos*. Augustine's commentaries on the Psalms have been utilized as a source both for information on liturgy (together with his *Sermones*)[17] and for reconstructing how psalmody was practised at Hippo and then Carthage after his return to Africa.[18] In the musicological literature, they turn up as an historical resource, helpful when it comes to seeking out descriptions of ancient musical instruments and for establishing the organological significance of ancient terms. To this end, Augustine's commentaries on the Psalms perform a similar service to the *Etymologiae* of Isidore of Seville. From a more philosophical angle, they have been used in the study of jubilation and of music number symbolism.[19] Rarest of all, though – and another reason for this book – has been any attention given in musicology today to the musical symbolism at work in Augustine's commentaries.[20] Once again, I want to stress that this is because this musical symbolism in Augustine's hands is, fundamentally, a challenge to the traditional methods of knowledge in the West and especially to the traditional methods of the historian in the West, which otherwise and necessarily come to direct our approach to a figure from so far back in the past as Augustine, notwithstanding whether we set out with the best of intentions and whether we set out to approach him from standpoints which are genuinely philosophical, aesthetical, ethical, metaphysical or psychological, as I listed them earlier. By now, and with so much known and documented, humanities disciplines have almost by default become taught and learnt as 'the history of' their subjects. This is not their fault. This is simply the difference between Augustine's day, when so much lay open to him and waiting to be discovered, and our day, when everything in between has been written up in books. To Augustine, writing and books – and most especially, then, his commentaries on the Psalms – were an act of engaging with the future rather than the past. The Psalmist was expressing something in order to light a fire in his hearers. From there, grace and the supernatural were expected to take over. Augustine felt the same way, and tried to replicate then this effect in his commentaries; and even of course, then, to amplify it. His idea was to use words, and more specifically, the images made out of words, to touch something off in his readers. But at the point of touch-off, control was then ceded to God, so that what happened next would be between God and the person touched. I repeat, in front of Augustine lay the mysterious future and the mysterious connections yet to be made between God and his (Augustine's) readers. What might prevent these connections being made was that the words and what they were saying become more significant than their symbolism. This is what the Psalmist himself seems to have understood and to have taken measures against. And Augustine admired what he saw and took his cue from him. Here, then, was an intimate relationship between the Christians' praise of their God and music – one which was founded upon a desire (in Augustine's case, certainly) to mark the point at which Christian wisdom overbounds Classical gnosis and rationality and departs for the occult, in which no one single meaning can exist to tie anything down. From the same one set of sounds, or words or images, God speaks differently to each. This must be a departure also, then, from faith or morality, traditionally conceived, or from all other codes of life.

Thus liberated into the full-bore esotericism of Augustine's wild side, it is time to disappear into his texts and 'play the game' with him.

[*Editor:* But not before Laurence has provided you, the reader, as promised, with something of a map, both to her ways in to the text, and through it, and then to her ways out, and to some of the implications for musicology, philosophy and Christian theology.]

ABBREVIATIONS

Abbreviations of Augustine's works cited in this book

Confess.	The *Confessions*
Contra Prisc. et Orig.	*Against the Priscillianists and the Origenists*
De civ. Dei	*The City of God*
De Mag.	*On the Teacher*
De mus.	*On music*
De ord.	*On order*
De Trin.	*On the Trinity*
De vera rel.	*On the true religion*
En.	*Expositions on the Psalms*
Ep.	*Letters*
Imm. an.	*The immortality of the soul*
In Io. Ev.	*Treatises on the Gospel of John*
Serm.	*Sermons*

Introduction, or first steps in to the text(s)

The musical image

Musical images appear across a diversity of contexts and are therefore subject to a variety of definitions, all of which complement each other. To the literal, presented images of the kind that we find in iconography to the written kind that we find in discourse in the form of metaphor and allegory, can be added the sensible images of music-making and the spiritual images of musical experience. All of these together we say form the imaginative musical journey of an epoch and a culture. While over and above all of this again, floats the fact and the question of *symbolism*.

First, however, I want to talk for a little while about musical images in terms of evocation and memory; for these two dimensions of human experience seemed to hold a particular fascination for Augustine and indeed would go on to give the character to what we might call his 'theory' of perception and to the great role and respect he gave to the human powers of creation in the act of perception. What this means is that there is a downgrading in Augustine of the communicating medium; viz., of words. Nowadays, this is very much what gives his thoughts on this subject their 'wildness', as I put it. Or frankly, their supernaturalism. For Augustine, words and all communicating media – music especially, then – are merely the triggers for living, roaming human minds. These minds are kept separate from each other by the principal fact that no one mind can ever enter into another. It becomes then, in fact, this impossibility, that makes communication and language and expression necessary in the first place, as Augustine sees it. Nowadays, we have become used in the West at least, to the scientific paradigm of truth and perception, in which the human mind does not have this principal role and mystery about it but is itself included as an item within the universe of the totality of facts. Within this scheme, the truth is what is actually empirically 'out there' and able to be taken hold of and catalogued by the methods of science. This is the same thing as to say that what happens inside a human mind in order to constitute what we mean by a 'human mind' within this scheme today is just as much subject to the laws of science as anything else that exists. We say that it is 'psychological', and mean the above. Augustine can of course be impressively psychological himself, when it comes to the ways and byways of the human will – his own especially and famously. However, when it comes to the questions and problems of 'mind' – to the philosophy of mind – he belongs to an outlook prepared to take solipsism deadly seriously. Right the way, in fact, to suggesting that whatever it is of 'truth' that one mind can communicate to another by means of media has so much to overcome on the face of it, that it must surely and ultimately rely on grace, or in his famous formulation and conclusion from his book on this subject, *De magistro*, 'Christ the interior teacher'. This puts Augustine squarely into the company of modern philosophers of language and most of all into the company of the most radical of them, Ludwig Wittgenstein. Like Wittgenstein, Augustine's outlook eventually paints a scene in which formalism and logic, progress and technology increasingly take care of themselves such that the human mind, its imagination and make-believe, becomes our only hope against them.[1]

According to Augustine, the images of things formed within us, interiorly, by means of words, can be divided between those that are 'fantastic' – that is, images generated mentally from a worded description of a thing of which the perceiving mind has had prior experience and therefore knows already – and those that are 'phantasms' – that is, images generated mentally of things never before seen and experienced, and therefore unknown.[2] This means that we can speak, really, of 'sonorous images' – images that, sparked by sound or symbol (on the outside), live out their lives freely, in our interior, mental, spiritual deeps. Naturally, this same process plays itself out spectacularly in music. Melodies show themselves to possess an occult affinity to the full spectrum of human affections, transmitting these affections to the listener and imprinting a sonorous image upon the memory which is itself then transformed in recollection.³

Music does not just generate images 'in time' with itself, so to speak, while we are listening, but proves itself especially well adapted to hanging around afterwards and eternally. Think of the difference between recalling a page of writing and its effect upon you and a passage of music. This is what I mean. There is no denying that relative to the page of words, the passage of music is unrestricted in its recollection. To recall a sequence of words takes one back into time: they must be sounded out in the mind all over again in exactly the sequence of the first time, or their meaning and evocation are lost. Not so a passage of music. It does not require to put us back into time in order to work its magic. Instead, it seems to float before us in some place outside of time – the wondrous place that Augustine reserved (again and again across his writings) for the human memory.⁴

This is to say that, in order to be able to understand what it was that we managed to hear in the fleeting flash of music that was then devoured by the same time which was required for its making, we must turn from the music itself and take up instead with the image of it that, not kept within fleeing time but in the always-present of the memory, is a place of impressions and feelings that we may wander in and out of at will and return to forever more. In this sense and clearly, we are talking of a process which to Augustine at least – and for being spiritual and interior and subject to the mysterious workings of the spirit and grace – represented an altogether superior form of understanding and knowledge to that transacted externally and empirically, in slavish and meticulous obedience to temporal reality.

This also made the musical image irresistible to being thought of and studied according to the 'trinity' of its relationship to reason, memory and will and thereby to past, present and future and to the actual Trinity of Christian doctrine. To give just one example, the man who conserves within his memory in the way above, an entire passage of music, might be said to be mimicking in a fractional way the otherwise inapproachable perspective of the Eternal Creator, in which past, present and future are indeed known by him in the entirety of their passage, although in some way which does not then affect him by return, as in the case of human emotion.[5]

For all of this, the musical image also turns around and becomes symbolic, as we have intimated. Beyond ordinary description, it can be carried by a variety of literary devices, chief amongst which allegory and metaphor. Up to the beginning of the modern period, analogy, the founding principal of metaphor, enjoyed an epistemological importance in general, and a status, that the rising Cartesian method then did a good deal to erode. Within Christian thought, the analogy, the metaphor, the allegory and the symbol had always had a particular role of first significance. This role and its significance came of course from the biblical text itself, and were then formalized by the Church Fathers. Because of this, its Christian ring-fencing, it would endure through the cultural changes of the modern period, the Cartesian revolution included.

According to a lovely expression of Augustine's, God plays with man by placing images within his sacred text and does not hesitate from using parables, allegories and metaphors to instruct him.[6] To this end, the images he uses do not have a decorative or recreative purpose, but a didactive one. In fact, the image is a cognitive means to drawing close to the Divine essence. In the Word, is seen a mirror to the Invisible. That is to say, God is not 'seen' in this mirror but they who look see instead his reflections in Sacred Scripture and in created reality. This use of the image as a means to Divine knowledge invokes the Pauline principal of anagogic reasoning, where the things invisible are seen within the mirror of the things visible.[7] In the course of this book, we will be seeing how this operates within the ambit of music and why Augustine should be considered one of the true masters of this 'technique' (if that is word) of theological-musical analogy. We will be analysing how he uses music to resolve theological questions and, vice versa, how he interrogates music by means of the elements of theology.

Within the Augustinian texts, analogy – the founder and fertilizer of reflection in all fields of understanding – gains a notable conceptual depth of weight, plus a theoretical structure and a maximal cultural density. It becomes the key to turning his philosophical and theological reasoning upon the very, and fundamental questions that same reasoning poses, and presupposes. And let me say also that to enter via Augustine into this 'world of analogy' is also to enter then into the wider world of analogy that guided and shaped the story of understanding – also, of scientific understanding – up to the late Renaissance. For Augustine excelled in analogy and was admired for it by those who knew. We say that from experience and intuition is born a scintilla that connects things and clarifies them in the gleam of a moment, in the mystical moment that sees everything yet leaves behind it only the trace of what it saw – but a trace nonetheless, in which is conserved the true density of everything.

The image as a mode of knowledge really does then find one of its particular forms of expression in the kaleidoscope of musical analogies, metaphors and allegories designed by Augustine, and arising from his long study of the Bible and his personal experience of music. These musical images, analogies, metaphors and allegories work to multiple purposes and participate at various levels of discourse, from anthropological to philosophical to theological. They also evolve from allegory to symbol. Not only does Augustine seem incapable of trusting a musical image with a merely decorative task, but he treats every such image as polyvocal and its polysemy is developed by him in all its possibilities and ramifications. In his biblical exegesis, he is always on the lookout for multiple senses of single words, and his interpretations of musical images are really just the great example of this.

These musical images acquire a symbolic dimension, not only because their allegorical interpretations overbound the literal sense of the text and of the single word, but because Augustine will tend to offer a variety of allegorical interpretations of each musical image. In this way, a single image may contain a plurality of significations and in its polysemy, it 'dresses' itself in the profundity of the symbol. The musical image points beyond itself and this other that it points to, is never banal. For Augustine, it is always to the divine mysteries and to the true nature of man. In this way also, then, is seen the peculiarity of the musical image over other available forms of metaphor and analogy.

[*Editor:* When I heard Laurence explain it to me like this, I thought of the following. Music aside, to work in words, whether by analogy or by metaphor or by allegory, is, just that, when you think about it – It is, still, to 'work in words.' That is, the work that one is doing never leaves the words, or moves outside them. The sensation is given, of having done so. But this is quite different to the real thing. Laurence's contention in this book in league with Augustine, is that only music affords you the *real thing*. Again, music aside, analogy, metaphor and allegory depend upon the prior, literal, intended meaning. The apparent flight into fantasy then made upon that meaning is not really then a flight into fantasy, if it all along has had the raison d'être of reinforcing that prior meaning. Literary devices are in this way, really, just exactly always that (*devices*) – They work by mechanical linkage to an original, pinned meaning that must hold fast lest the entire system of extended meaning connected to it collapse into free-floating meaninglessness. Literary devices may therefore be clever and even beautiful, but above all what we admire in them is their ingenuity; plus the side of the human brain which this ingenuity reveals in action. The human brain is capable of presenting and representing reality to itself and others until at last the penny drops. The most complicated theorem of science may thus be explained to a child eventually by means of bread rolls and sugar shakers moved about on a table-top. Or the deepest psychology may turn up in a dream as flowers and flying saucers. But notice then that all of this depends upon some empirical reality – whether in the world about us or in the world inside us – that stands in need of explanation. But the introduction of music, or the turn to it, really does seem to change this; or perhaps better said, to destroy it. To destroy the system of it. If in conventional literary devices, you move farther and farther away from something in order the better to see it, or in order at last to see it, with music, *it sees you*. You straightaway find that you have ceded control to it because the reality it works upon is you (who is now shown to stand in need of explanation). And how different a situation that is to the traditional semiotics of a language (game). Music plays you. If it is sad, then its sadness is felt through some sadness of yours which it calls forth and accompanies. And likewise for the other person, or the other people, listening. In this way, a sad piece of music is sad not because of some single sadness in the world which it points to but because of its unerring ability to evoke an original sadness in each and every listener. Words work by pointing us ultimately – directly and indirectly – to some reality, sufficiently stable to be seen alike by all. They work by requiring from us a basic obedience to their call. They work if we do what they say. They line us up on the parade ground. They generate the (ethical) imperative to do this. Music, on the other hand, shows us sadness (or whatever else) in its infinite conceivable varieties; these varieties depending, in turn, upon the infinity of possible listeners. In this way, music proves to be naturally resistant to the doctrinaire forms of knowledge and truth which treat humankind on the basis of its biological and medical uniformity and consistency and naturally attentive, instead, to the whole other dimension of human life, which is characterized by the fact of how each of us navigates our way according to a unique set of responses, feelings, dreams, fears, and so on.[8] Augustine thus found music and musical symbolism to be peculiarly well adapted to his own preferences when articulating Christianity. Namely, that a life should be examined down to the point of its utter distinction and separation from all other lives (*Confessiones*) only to meet the God who is then and somehow also all things to all people, all of the time (*De Trinitate*).]

The reconstitution of the symbolic polysemy of the metaphorical and allegorical uses of music by Augustine results, then, in a painting, in which all dimensions – anthropological, theological, philosophical and musical – interweave at once and indissolubly and are impossible, on the face of it, to un-weave. Music is seen to resolve or clarify certain enigmas, to talk of themes fundamental to present and future life or to approach to the profound impenetrability of the Mystery. From the purpose of human life on earth to the mystery of the Passion, from hope in the resurrection to the way to the house of our Father in Heaven, music assumes always the privileged role. To look in the mirror of philosophical and theological texts is to see musical images both in their symbolical value and in their speculative content and potential. The point that I am trying to make here – and once again the magic of music in the hands of a writer and mystic like Augustine – is that all of this proves immune to scholarly reduction in the traditional way. To enter into Augustine's texts, as I have done; to stay true to him in analysing and assembling his achievement; is to be left at the end of it all with something as alive and evangelical as at the beginning. Scholarly reduction is meant to kill and then dissect in order to do properly its work of cutting out passion and subjectivity and laying out the facts on the table. But with Augustine, and with Augustine and music, the body rises again and dances off in to the night! The original mission and message remain as strong and clear as ever!

The 'musical man'

Augustine speaks of music both at the personal level – just remember how his conversion begins, in effect, from a musical act[9] – and at the theoretical level. At the theoretical level, music, whether practical or speculative, resolves the more complex questions that he encounters: just remember the role of musical analogy in his speculations on the enigma of Creation.[10] But over and above these, there is a particular and very special musical image: that of the 'musical man' (*l'uomo musicale*).

The figure of the musical man, or as we might sometimes speak of him in this book, the 'man of music', runs right the way through the cultural history of Europe. There already in the literature of Classical Greece – in Plato's *Phaedo*, for example (85e) – and in the first centuries before Christ, one can trace a coherent Judeo-Christian tradition working itself out in works of theology, musical theory, philosophy and medicine – all the way up to the end of the seventeenth century. Augustine will theorize certain characteristics of this man, transforming him from an essentially Platonic creation into a Christian one. This Christianization of the Platonic tradition will see the advent, yes, of a new man, his ancient characteristics enriched and remade according to the burgeoning Christian culture. The man of music, made in the image of God, will become a resonant being, a receptacle of the Divine Word, possessed thereby of a new song and of a new and special relationship to the Father, most particularly when (in the Augustinian imagination) the Father sings and plays in order to attract to himself the soul of this new man (in order to make him new in the first place). It is true to say that it is only in the bosom of this image of the musical man that the Christian specifics of the whole rest of Augustine's musical imagery fully offers itself, and that we get to see in full evidence the originality of Augustine's musical thought.

The idea of man as made in God's image is always thought of in connection with the word and the limitations of the word as we have talked of them thus far. This might be the greatest example, then, of Augustine's ability to see original sin and human fallenness everywhere at work. So, in 'the word' of man is seen an image at least, of *The Word* of God; except that now (down here) it is bound up with temporality and must be expressed by means of temporal extension in metred-out words, songs, sounds and silences. It is in the image of God, yes, and we are speaking of an absolute connection of kind. Yet because this is Augustine, we are also always talking of an absolute category of difference described by the fall of man. A difference between two cities. For Augustine, then, it is also the paradigm of what Christ had to clothe himself in as God-made-man. Plus the mystery of it, in the sense of how he was able to become incarnate and to enter fully and authentically into the beat of human life, feeling and fearing things as they came towards him from afar. Musical instruments are of course also then involved in the drama and plot of the musical man, in particular the stringed instruments, insofar as they speak (melodiously) to the heart. This heart, along with reason, mind, intellect, soul and body all participate in the musical metaphors associated with this man and his transformation by grace and Augustine's commentaries on the Psalms (noted for their constant dialogue between the two Testaments, Old and New; that is, between the 'Former' and the 'Reformer', the Word of Creation and the Saving Word, the Ancient Law and the New Law) are where the real action takes place. Augustine's great work and effort in commentating these 150 Psalms give us the man of music in all his fullness and possibly, in his best and clearest articulation in history. Yet not gifted to us on a plate! No, but fragmented and dispersed across the full 150 and awaiting our reconstruction of him.

This reconstruction which the study of Augustine allows for shows to us the man of music in all his faces. He is at once 'the faith' (in fact the musical man will become for Augustine the paradigm of the good Christian and will achieve then in new Christian form the Platonic ideal of properly tempered nature), the prophet, the saint and the Christ (in his incarnate, human nature). Each of these faces displays a particular relationship to music, the characteristics of which musical allegory and metaphor serve to define.

The investigation presented here in this book departs from man and from Christ – understood in his sensible musical dimensions – and arrives at the Father – understood in his super-sensible musical dimensions. Along the way, the musical man, so central to musical thinking and history in the West, is rediscovered and defined along new lines (i.e. those represented by the Christianization of Platonic thought). The journey moves from corporeal sound to incorporeal sound and reaches therefore the final point and object of all Augustinian reflection upon music, which being the 'ineffable music' and the 'silence' that is not then a mathematical or numbered music, intelligible on that basis, but a music that integrates the qualitative dimensions of sound and replays the aesthetic and mystical memory of musical experience.

In his commentaries on the Psalms, Augustine presents a God who actually himself does sing and play and wittingly and unwittingly, then, contrasts him with the Platonic musical demiurge (who performs these activities on behalf of the highest Being for whom they would otherwise be demeaning; so to speak). This should remind us once again of Augustine's determination to use music to illustrate the *likeness* between created man and Creator God, and to pursue this over and against the gigantic temptation of Platonism, which is simply to offer explanation of those features of the universe that stand to reason. Included in these then, by necessity and famously, is the world of ideas: whose inclusion by necessity becomes also then its 'proof'. To Plato, music represents an essential rationality in the universe to which man can and should be attuned. To Augustine, on the other hand, it represents the extent to which God is genuinely lovable and praiseworthy and approachable, even if he is at the same time truly God and therefore – technically – 'inhuman'. Again, Plato's God is at best admirable and extremely jolly clever on the evidence of all that he has made and its intricate order. And music – mathematical music – becomes the final evidence and point of our highest participation in that order. Whereas Augustine's God is capable, it seems, of taking a pleasure in his work *similar* to the pleasure that we can take in it looking on. There is always, between us and him, an insurmountable difference of kind, yet, there is always this similarity of pleasure and joy. Thus, in the Augustinian scheme, God is musical, and so are we; with the difference of kind between him and us being that his music is properly *Ineffable* while ours only approximates to ineffability.

> [*Editor:* Time for another quick intervention, because Laurence is pursuing and marking a critical distinction that plays throughout her text, but which takes us into the realms of deep

mysticism. I think she means this. At least, this is how I have always understood it. The Platonic universe is always – when you think about (excuse the pun) – a *described* universe. It is always being thought about and written about by at least one human being, with the whole force of Platonism following from that. In other words, because it is such as that we can think and write about it in the way that we can, it is a rational universe plotted by a rational deity. This is the same thing as to say that between this rational deity and our rational selves, stretches something that is unbroken and can be moved about at will by the properly trained mind. We can designate this unbrokenness by numbers or music or some other derivative that stays true to it. It doesn't matter by this point. What matters is the unbrokenness plus the whole ethic of the good life that rapidly assembles on top of it, and which inevitably gives pride of place to the function of mind, and how mind can both see and follow the patterns of this unbrokenness (and *should then* see and follow them – The Socratic imperative). To Augustine, these patterns and laws exist and are true as far as they go – and as far as he was concerned, the Platonic description of them was as good as any – however, his interest and concern and excitement, it seems, was to locate and argue for the *brokenness* that must be there to signify the difference between Creator and creature and which doubly-must be there in a postlapsarian world. If I understand it correctly, Laurence's argument, on Augustine's behalf, is that music – alone of all the arts – seeks for this same brokenness and calls us to love it. That in fact, this brokenness is the reason that we can love God in the first place and call upon him (grace notwithstanding). Like everything else in this world, music is logically and historically determinate; and can be taught and learnt as an art because of this. Yet unlike the other arts, which connect themselves to us and God on one unbroken plane, music *is* the break and the breakaway – It is the point at which an activity within this world and following its rules yet takes flight from them. It is then body *and soul*; except again, not the described soul of Platonism. It is the soul that truly does escape the rules and that lives by escaping them. This truth, which remains inadmissible and paradoxical within Platonism, becomes the touchstone of Augustinianism; especially the mature Augustinianism of Augustine's commentaries on the

Psalms. We see it in other mature works, like in *De civitate Dei*.[11] Hence Augustine's tendency to focus on songs without words, or the purely instrumental sound; his definition of the ineffability of music as because of its purpose as a fitting response to *The Ineffable*; and his theorising of the specifics of divine music.]

The edifice of sound

The concatenation of musical notions developed by Augustine can trace its origins to the importance he places upon *rhythm*. Rhythm seems to possess its own proper reason which the universe follows. Think only of the song of the nightingale[12] or of the rooster,[13] or observe the forwards motion of the worm and the rhythm in that.[14] Together with the universe, Augustine will also Christianize the platonic Soul, conserving its incorruptible perfection of number: that is, God eternal lays within the soul the rhythm of wisdom and this rhythm carries the soul back to him and to the original rhythm that resides in him.

First there was rhythm. Time measured in beats of the heart, in a pass, in two bodies moving voluptuously together – and therefore in harmony and love's embrace.[15] The rhythms of created reality define the musical rationality of universal harmony and place it in movement. From that beating heart to every other thing that moves in the universe – from the steps of ants to the courses of planets – all of it gives testimony not just to the mathematical rationality of reality, but to the (supernatural) fact of the passing of time. The things of reality cannot be unless they are in time, but time passes and cannot itself be stopped (which is strange, when we think about it).

If time cannot be stopped, it can at least be measured, thanks to choreography, to poetry and to music and to the arts that impress an order on to time's continuous flow.[16] The measurement of time is an urgent and essential question for Augustine.[17] It is because to his reckoning, everything is all-the-time fleeing, right the way to the fact that you start to wonder whether you can rightly consider that things exist – right the way to considering whether even man himself exists, if the truth is that everything is in the constant business of disappearing. And yet, in time and because of time, one gets to witness also the beauty of things in their coming and going, moment by moment, in that rhythmic movement signified by the rationality of number.[18]

From the rationality of rhythm, it is possible to arrive at and think upon the rationality and therefore also the value of *pure sound*, of sound without words. In this study, we will see how Augustine can take this principal to its extreme logical conclusion. This valorization of sound – in obvious distinction to his infamous reacting to melodies in the context of Church music (as distracting from the sacramentality of the words), already mentioned by us – must be understood within a wider discourse of Augustine's on mystical nature. This discourse, and Augustine's thinking on pure sound, will go on to influence a good part of the theological tradition to follow him. Witness, for example, Bernard of Clairvaux's theory of affective language, and how he was to argue its superiority over the rational language of logical argumentation.[19] Theology aside, it will also go on to figure in musical theory proper and in repeating debates on the hierarchy between instrumental music and voice. This question of the opposition and/or the complementarity between the singing voice and the accompanying, instrumental sound you can also find being approached directly on occasion, in some of Augustine's commentaries on the Psalms. In addition to the rationality of pure sound resulting from rhythm, we will get to see also the sense in which this pure sound will acquire a semantics of its own and proper to itself: one that is revealed through theological-musical analogy and metaphor on the inspiration of the images presented in Scripture.

The qualitative dimension of music – the description of the quality of sound and not just of the sonorous quantity of the ratio of the intervals – is something that should be considered in parallel with the attention that is given to the relationship between music and *affect*. The connection between affect and music one finds displayed in Augustine's writings under various aspects. Here, in this study, we will zoom out somewhat from the notorious passage in the tenth book of his *Confessiones*, already cited by us a number of times, in which Augustine underlines the occult affinity between music and the entire range of human affections, and pursue a more independent and indirect exploration of the extent to which the link between music and affect may be significant rather as the place where the particularity of the Christian message gets confused with the specifics of musical language. This brings us up to the notion of musical experience, or the experience of music.

Experience is the foundation of Augustine's entire philosophical endeavour, let alone his articulation of music. Behind all his reflections on music, as their basis, is the single fact that he himself had made the experience of being rapt by music, of allowing it to invade him. And the episode in Book Ten of his *Confessiones*, when he was brought to tears by those Church melodies, was not to be the only time this happened – the only time he was to be so rapt. No, he was to be similarly affected – and his theoretical speculations were to be similarly affected – by the practice of the singing of the Psalms. Augustine simply would never have become the investigator superior of the minutiae of the human psyche had he not begun with (his own) experience, both sensible and spiritual. Likewise, he simply would never have developed his theories on listening and on sound, on the suavity and sweetness of musical instruments and song, had he not first allowed himself to be their direct object and subject. One reads often in his commentaries on the Psalms how the singing of the same is helping the meditative reflections on that which is being sung; that in fact, singing *is* thinking in this case; that meditation and understanding have become synonymous. In this way, the saintly words melt with the song and it is this melting that makes them the means of spiritual comprehension and that makes them capable of bearing theological interpretations.

We might say that sensible experience gets consumed by spiritual understanding, and that this constitutes one of the nodes of Augustinian musical thinking. Music brings Augustine to a place whence he is overtaken like Saint Paul was overtaken (and Paul is, of course, everywhere in Augustine's writing) by a supernatural voice. The musical experience returns him to himself – deep into himself – where there is discovered another music, a *silent* music, which becomes to him the height and perfection of his spiritualism and his theology.

That the musical experience is in this way at once sensible and spiritual points us to another critical feature of Augustinian thought. But one which for its mysticism, asks a lot of us in a book, at second-hand. But then this is why, when it comes to it (very soon!), we are going to jump into the text with Augustine, and see if we can bypass those limitations. When it comes to the question and process of the human perception of holy, or 'invisible', or supernatural things –

which was a question put repeatedly to Christian intellectuals like Augustine – and when music was then brought in by him to be the example – it always went as follows. The sensible, transporting experience of music was said to issue in the mysterious silent music, or music of silence, of above. The musical silence becoming then the same thing as the formal theory of 'musical ineffability', or music as formally and best representing ineffability. Ineffability, meanwhile, being the intrinsically Divine feature from the point of view of existence. Existence, in turn, viz., materiality, or sensibility, being the chief point of view of the educated pagan opponents of early Christianity (witness Paul's countering of Stoic and Epicurean views in the Scriptures) and Christianity in Augustine's day, and Augustine's Christianity in particular (see how he puts it in his letter 118 to Dioscorus, which mentions Paul[20]). We can put it again by saying that here, in this book, our journey will end at the point at which we stand before the ineffability of human music on the one hand, and on the other hand, before the ineffable music of God. In both cases, thought is reduced to silence.

[*Editor:* Laurence continues to move on a high plain here and I want to give general readers a chance to think their way through the mechanics which lead up to this point. This will also, I hope, be of help to professional philosophers and theologians and Augustine specialists not familiar with the special considerations and opportunities that music brings to the table in discussions of the Christian God's omniscience. In doing this, and in the interests of fairness, I will make use only of ground we have covered to this point in this book. In Augustine's mature opinion, Platonism is the pagan philosophy that most closely approximates to Christian doctrine and Christian creed. However, to Augustine, close – even here 'most closely' – always means 'close, but no cigar'. This is because the Platonists, in not acknowledging Christ (and the New Testament), do not acknowledge grace. Even Christians who stray similarly into not acknowledging Christ and grace, become for Augustine heretics on that account. As, most famously, with Pelagius. The reason why – the reason why it is always in this matter for Augustine, 'close, but no cigar' – is because grace is supernatural. It represents God's, in Christ's, utterly mysterious work and utter freedom of action in eternity. As he will put it: 'The Holy

Ghost blows where he will [John 3.8]. He does not follow men's merits, but actually produces them himself. For the grace of God is extinct unless it be totally free.' What this means, is that Grace has, quite categorically, nothing to do with worded, defined, doctrine or creed. These formulas are *geometrically* true, and therefore they allow the Christian to *speak* correctly of his God. But if speaking correctly of God were the way to get to Heaven, then Platonism would be sufficient; in fact, it would be more than sufficient, given its intellectual sophistication and breadth of coverage vis-à-vis the Christian Scriptures. No, for Augustine, this potential intellectual self-sufficiency of philosophy always amounted to 'pride', and was therefore the great danger to be guarded against. But it did set up an intriguing problem that would need until the 20th century to come to prominence; and which perhaps we only now see fully in the 21st, when science can offer such a total picture of the universe. What science and rationalism and therefore Platonism could impress upon Augustine in his day, and therefore all the more magnificently and forcefully now, in ours, is that, notwithstanding the language of omniscience and ineffability, when God speaks and acts in history, then even he – that is, his speech and action – must become subject to the physical laws of such things (in order to be considered speech and action in the first place). Furthermore, these laws are what Western Science counts as knowledge and tabulates and teaches as knowledge and then also truth and *Final Truth*. In relation to this, chaos and flux and happenstance is merely apparent, because there is always a level (nowadays, the atomic, or even the sub-atomic level) at which everything that happens can be seen to be the example of these invariable laws in action. Augustine's warning, then, is that if Christian theology is not careful, it can slip (through pride, always through pride) into the system of acquiring knowledge of God by means of the scientific analysis of his speech and actions in history. This system of knowledge may even then be used to challenge God Himself; if, say, he were to say or do something contrary to the laws and patterns established in his name (in doctrine and creed). The only way out of this, is to let speech be speech, and acts be acts, and the laws be the laws, and doctrine be doctrine, but to set against it then by definition, the freedom of God, the freedom of Christ, the freedom of Grace, and the freedom of the Holy Ghost. This freedom is what Paul meant when he set the Spirit against the letter. And this freedom is exactly what Augustine saw the chance to express, *in musical symbolism.* Just think about it. When Plato and Pythagoras and all the great thinkers of antiquity so inclined desired to finger the pulse of existence, they went to music. For music is the one human art that absolutely depends upon the laws of the universe and their numbers to be, and to be made. It was discovered in its magical intervals and ratios, as its magical intervals and ratios, and cannot depart from them; lest it cease to be music at all. It is the only art which for all of this does leave behind it a trail which can be perfectly followed to the same conclusion. It is the only art which can be scored. It is the only art which possesses the consistencies (the ratios and intervals) to be scored; score in this case referring quite directly to number. You could not have stood by Picasso and scored his painting and handed the sheet on afterwards to another painter sufficiently trained, and watch them produce the same result. But music is so magically mathematical, that you can. In fact, so true is this magic, and so true to nature, that you can use nature – mechanically – to play music back. As music can be scored on paper for the human eye, so too can it be grooved into vinyl for the stylus. The function of the playback becoming then proof of the unerring interconnectedness of everything in the universe. Music shows this to us, and shows it to us best, and has always been venerated by the wise for it. It taps and displays to us the mesmerizing feature of the universe, which being that nothing may take place outside of its laws. The Christian is obliged to venerate it as the wonder of God's design; and indeed, even the recorded miracles of the Christian religion do not subvert these laws but work with them in new and surprising ways. (For example, even the turning back of time is still 'the turning back of time'. That is, it can sensibly be described as that. It is an incredible accomplishment, but yet it is an accomplishment nonetheless, made wondrous to us, and miraculous to us when we think about it, by its logicality. Miracles are miraculous because they are seen for what they are. Otherwise, they would pass unnoticed.) AND YET, for all of this – for being so rigidly the letter and the law – music is at exactly the same time the Spirit!

Again, to compose it and to play it, one has to follow the laws of the universe to the letter, yet it is vaunted – and truly vaunted – as the one experience that can bring us out on *Silence*, and silence's freedom of thought. Music becomes therefore the perfect representation and the perfect symbol, of the God who on the one hand created this universe with a goodness that is expressed in its eternal rhythms, but on the other hand who can and does act and will in all directions, in a way that can only be depicted (I earlier said 'defined') against such rhythms, as freedom's silence. This is music's mystical aspect to which Laurence refers. And its value and allure today, is the same as it was in Augustine's day. I can think of one delightful example in a letter Augustine wrote in 415 to Evodius, a long-time member of his intellectual circle and fellow protagonist. In it, he mentions Gennadius, a noted man of medical science whose doubts about the life after death were resolved in a dream involving music. Everything that I have just spoken of is present in this letter in abundance. There is Augustine's bemusement and dismay at how men will rate and pursue as knowledge the general-case laws of the universe and do nothing on their own behalf. By this he means, here, and always, the mysterious, evidently immaterial position taken up by our *Self*. In a universe which is otherwise lawful, and manifestly so, our human selves disobey all of its laws in order merely to be and to produce in us even the most trifling of thoughts, memories, revelations, and so on. In a word, *Consciousness*. To a medical man like Gennadius, consciousness, and the extension of consciousness into the life after death, become a hard teaching to accept. Hard, because medical science and the long experience of it will otherwise show an intelligent man the counter-truth that the laws and their materiality cannot be withstood. What will tip the balance in the example of Gennadius, is a dream; but not any old dream. Dreams of course of their own should cause us sufficient wonder and prove consciousness, but Augustine is sympathetic to the cumulative effect on the brain of the repeating drumbeat of science. So, Gennadius experiences not any-old dream, the repetition of his waking world, but a dream in which are heard and therefore experienced – and by that, Augustine means *truly* experienced, and the supernaturality of that therefore – the very hymns of praise of the saints in Heaven.

For my part, as I discover more plainly my inability to account for the ordinary facts of our experience, when awake or asleep, throughout the whole course of our lives, the more do I shrink from venturing to explain what is extraordinary. For while I have been dictating this epistle to you [Evodius], I have been contemplating your person in my mind – you being, of course, absent all the while, and knowing nothing of my thoughts – and I have been imagining from my knowledge of what is in you how you will be affected by my words; and I have been unable to apprehend, either by observation or by inquiry, how this process was accomplished in my mind. Of one thing, however, I am certain, that although the mental image was very like something material, it was not produced either by masses of matter or by qualities of matter … I will narrate briefly, however, one fact which I commend to your meditation. You know our brother Gennadius, a physician, known to almost every one, and very dear to us, who now lives at Carthage, and was in other years eminent as a medical practitioner at Rome. You know him as a man of religious character and of very great benevolence, actively compassionate and promptly liberal in his care of the poor. Nevertheless, even he, when still a young man, and most zealous in these charitable acts, had sometimes, as he himself told me, doubts as to whether there was any life after death. Forasmuch, therefore, as God would in no wise forsake a man so merciful in his disposition and conduct, there appeared to him in sleep a youth of remarkable appearance and commanding presence, who said to him: 'Follow me.' Following him, he came to a city where he began to hear on the right hand sounds of a melody so exquisitely sweet as to surpass anything he had ever heard. When he inquired what it was, his guide said: 'It is the hymn of the blessed and the holy.' What he reported himself to have seen on the left hand escapes my remembrance. He awoke; the dream vanished, and he thought of it as only a dream. On a second night, however, the same youth appeared to Gennadius, and asked whether he recognised him, to which he replied that he knew him well, without the slightest uncertainty. Thereupon he asked Gennadius where he had become acquainted with him. There also his memory failed him not as to the proper reply: he narrated the whole vision, and the hymns of the saints which, under his guidance, he had been taken to hear, with all the readiness natural to recollection of some very recent experience. On this the youth inquired whether it was in sleep or when awake that he had seen what he had just narrated. Gennadius answered: 'In sleep.' The youth then said: 'You remember it well; it is true that you saw these things in sleep, but I would have you know that even now you are seeing in sleep.' Hearing this, Gennadius was persuaded of its truth, and in his reply declared that he believed it. Then his teacher went on to say: 'Where is your body now?' He answered: 'In my bed.' 'Do you know,' said the youth, 'that the eyes in this body of yours are now bound and closed, and at rest, and that with these eyes you are seeing nothing?' He answered: 'I know it.' 'What, then,' said the youth, 'are the eyes with which you see me?' He, unable to discover what to answer to this, was silent. While he hesitated, the youth unfolded to him what he was endeavouring to teach him by these questions, and immediately said: 'As while you are asleep and lying on your bed these eyes of your body are now unemployed and doing nothing, and yet you have eyes with which you behold me, and enjoy this vision, so, after your death, while your bodily eyes shall be wholly inactive, there shall be in you a life by which you shall still live, and a faculty of perception by which you shall still perceive. Beware, therefore, after this of harbouring doubts as to whether the life of man shall continue after death.' This believer says that by this means all doubts as to this matter were removed from him. By whom was he taught this but by the merciful, providential care of God?[21]]

Some hermeneutical considerations plus my new (old!) methodology

The thought of Augustine has nourished the religious literature on musical theory for centuries – and equally in the Protestant as in the Catholic worlds. To retrace and analyse music in Augustine's texts is to return oneself to the origin of a tradition that has continued down the centuries. To conduct a detailed reading of the Psalmodic instances of musical expression commentated on by Augustine is to enter into a precise understanding of the symbolical significance of the musical images deployed in those passages.

Augustine elaborates ideas that will be familiar to any who have studied the history of music, the philosophy of music and musical aesthetics. His definition of the beautiful and its criteria in the arts speaks for itself.[22] However, there are other just as important but lesser-known ideas with which his commentaries on the Psalms in particular can bring us into contact. Two of these would be the mystery of the origin of 'musical creation' (see section above, for what is meant by this) and the relationship between musical language and the *unsayable*. The Augustinian texts furnish a historical master key to studying the ineffability, the hearing (the 'heard dimension'), the sweetness and the harshness of sound; the value of musical instruments; and the emotions communed with by music. Their descriptions of the intimate experience of the ineffable afforded by music, of exterior and interior listening, sound and silence, of melodiousness both sensible and spiritual, offer to the reader of today a point of view on music at once anthropological, philosophical and theological. This is important because without the theological point of view, a great part of musical culture is lost to us as we lose the very literary setting in which music's original allegories played out. This loss of biblical literacy does equal damage to the philosophical aspects of musical culture, if we think only of the pre- and postlapsarian framework of Christian thought, and what we have already said so far as regards the difference between the Spirit and the Letter, or the music of the universe as numbers and science and the music of the universe as mysticism and wonder and the source of man's hymn of praise, by return, to God. As for the anthropological point of view, one cannot help but be struck, when reading Augustine, by its modernity. Augustine enters into the labyrinth of the human psyche and into the deepest known reaches of the human mind and the human senses, 'showing it back to itself', so to speak, as the intellect and heart in action upon, and in response to music. Augustine is exceptionally good at showing us, therefore, what really, actually happens when music encounters us and touches us. His exposition is never dry, but wet-through with examples drawn from his experience and by extension, then, from ours.

I want to make it clear that in this book, I focus, more or less, on Augustine's commentaries on the Psalms (*Enarrationes in Psalmos*). A separate musicological study on his sermons and letters (*Sermones* and *Epistolae*) remains by me in the planning stages.

The very number of the Psalms (150), including within them the gradual chants (15), has a symbolic sense which confers on the whole a unitary dimension.[23] The Psalms of David announce the New Testament and the King pre-announces Christ. The union of the Two Testaments exerts a constant pull of orientation on Augustine's comments:

> But that the number three has relation to the mind may be understood from this, that we are commanded to love God after a threefold manner, with the whole heart, with the whole soul, with the whole mind: of each of which severally we must treat, not in the Psalms, but in the Gospels.[24]

Augustine is fond of number analogies! The Decalogue along with the ten-corded psalter of David emblemizes the Law that Christ does bring to completion.[25] And it is because he perfects but does not consummate the Law, completes but does not consent to it, that Christ finishes the Psalms of David. Once again, we are reminded of the distinction that Augustine will insist must needs be kept, between eternal rhythms of the universe that are truly seen for what they are and cannot be altered and Christ and Grace and the Holy Ghost, who go where they will regardless, and whose freedom truly is, then, mysterious and miraculous. What we are referring to here is really the rule that has guided the interpretation of Scripture in general, and which Augustine follows faithfully: 'All the things written down from the date of God's creation may be interpreted as images of the future.'[26] That is again, as prefiguring Christ's mission.

In Augustine's commentaries on the Psalms, the dimension of *Song* is ever-present. From out of the text, sung of course before it is interpreted, is heard the voice of Christ and of the Church, the Head and the Body, the voice that announces and the voice that has come to complete the law, the voice that speaks for man and of man but together with man, and which makes truth from his words. Augustine's interpretations abound in musical metaphors, even in the case of Scriptural passages in which the musical dimension is not literally present. On the other hand, there are the Psalms in which music features intrinsically and explicitly. With these, Augustine always lays over an allegorical interpretation.

As I have been stressing throughout, to confront oneself with Augustine's texts is to enter into a school of methodology quite different to the modern historical or the modern musicological schools, arising, as they did, in the eighteenth century. Then, quite understandably, the excitement was to collect and 'discover'; perhaps even to be the first to discover something, anything. And the ethic that grew up to accompany this great (as it was then to become, Darwinian) effort to catalogue and display was the idea that one was making good on all the preceding centuries' neglect. Let us simply point out that all the last of their species in the eighteenth and nineteenth centuries were shot and then stuffed (for Science). When it comes to music of course, this approach was, is and continues to be(!) a little insensitive. Or ironic. For example, it still will rip through Augustine's commentaries on the Psalms and see nothing there but the scattered bones of fifth-century music and musicianship. It will reassemble them for what they are worth, then move on. The knowledge produced in this way is not untrue, and certainly it has its value for its picture of life back then. However, given the riches it passes over in silence, it is a bit like going to Degas for the ballet shoes, or to life-drawing for the giggles. It misses the point. Augustine's whole excitement in approaching the Christian Psalms through the ambit of music was to discover that the texts themselves began to repay him in the manner of music and that his own writing and commentaries on them began to do the same and to take on a life of their own.

> [*Editor:* Everything is suddenly connected, but not in the manner of scientific knowledge, in which it was connected anyway and all along – regardless of whether or not *we* see it – but in the eye of the beholder and in the *eye of the beholder alone*. This reproduces of its own accord then and exactly, the great question of Music – Or at any rate, the great question of Music as it has always appeared to me. Which being, 'Why do the notes, or tones, go together as they do in order to make it?' Which in keeping with the theme and outlook of this book, is as much as to say, 'Why do the atoms of the universe go together as they do in order to make it (and everything in it)?' Here we see also – yet again – why music makes for such great symbolism in these matters. Because it is categorical proof that certain combinations go well (on the ear), and others not. The scientific reduction of what is going on reveals numbers and patterns and produces then great excitement. But can this intellectual

understanding then circle back and produce music by return? Thanks to Arnold Schoenberg and the Second Viennese School, this would become one of the questions of musical composition and theory and of course aesthetics in the twentieth century. Up to that point, the question had not really presented itself. Music, and certainly classical music, had been pursued and composed and created according to the *ear*, and to what pleased the ear. It had been found that what pleased the composer's ear well enough tended also to please the ears of people at large. Meanwhile, whatever was pleasing and successful and beautiful on this basis was also found to be conforming to certain laws, such as *the tonal hierarchy* and *tonal harmonies*. This was taken to be the magic of the thing, and if you were Christian, the magic of the whole great ordering of a God-created universe plus the benefit in kind, of obeying it in music and art. What Schoenberg and the Second Viennese Circle asked was, 'What if a large part of this is really just a matter of taste and tradition?' Accordingly, new methods of composition were explored, the most famous of these becoming Schoenberg's twelve-tone method. What interests me, and my point here, is that these new methods, although calling down scorn and outright aggression in some cases from the various constituencies with vested interests in classical culture (the Nazis being the most extreme of these), were methods nonetheless. Of course, their sheer provocation tended to hide this, making it appear as though the movement were a wilful, 'punk' style of thing. A rejection of European Christian culture for its own sake. What lay at the heart of the movement, though, was a meticulous and brilliant understanding of the physics of music. Notes, or again tones, obey – *must obey* – just the same rule as every other thing that is considered discrete and defined within physics' theoretical universe. This rule says is that no one thing to be so considered may possess two quantities at once (that is, in the same moment of time). This rule gives us the series of natural numbers and allows us to count them out (whilst also making it that this series must stretch then to infinity). Likewise, it gives us the notes, or tones, of music, understood as possessing each of them, a definite sonic frequency, or pitch. A note is a note, and music as we know it and can hear it is music as we know it and can hear it because of this rule: again, that no two pitches may occupy the same space-moment. Of course two different pitches may occupy the same moment, as when both hands play together on the piano to strike up chords or indeed in the grand-scale case of an orchestra of different hands and instruments, but always the space-moments of each pitch remain discrete and defined, which the written-out musical scores and their scores of notes, show. I mention this last as a reminder that formal music, like formal number and like all else that can be compassed within physics' theoretical universe is less an accurate depiction of nature than a statement about how the human mind works, and must work. What physical theory and all other theory shows, is that we cannot take in the whole of everything in the eternal, God-like glance. Instead, our minds demand a picture made up of an infinity of those discrete, defined things. Discrete so that they may be counted one-at-a-time, defined so that their behaviour may be considered predictable when once our mind has to turn elsewhere and leave them be. Mathematics is the largest and most obvious example of what the human mind can then achieve if these conditions are absolutely met and if all numbers absolutely do not and ever misbehave. Music, though, is the more intriguing example (and philosophy has always felt this), because it includes all of this but adds in the contrivances called 'musical instruments', in which the greatest ingenuity is displayed in designing these machines in order to pluck out, or blow out or strike out single notes. Which brings me back to where I began this reflection and why I introduced Schoenberg. For Schoenberg did no more than to realize that if music is as obedient as mathematics, then why not a new method of composing it? For if this method were as legitimately to follow the rules of physics as the method(s) before it, then music would follow it out – Would have to follow it out (in the same way as numbers have to follow out the functions of mathematics). Thus came into being Schoenberg's twelve-tone method and its results. But then why the great fuss and consternation, from the Nazis on? Because it brought the Western mind, and Western aesthetics, back squarely to the question of *Beauty*; of the fitting and the meet. And because it touched on and exposed the great strangeness – or even the paradox – or possibly even the lesson – at the heart of it all. Music can be stopped in its tracks, can be shown a whole new method and be made to follow it; and the initiated and those with sufficient technical and intellectual understanding can follow it too in its results in performance; but the fact is that these results are otherwise underwhelming. Even if he did not intend to, Schoenberg put to the test whether the beauty and the pleasure of music is merely its mechanical consistency to itself or whether it is – in fact – nothing to do with music qua music but with what music reaches out to express. Namely, the unspeakable depths and heights of human emotion as well as the unspeakable human longing to burst the bounds of merely sensible reality and commune with that is beyond. At any rate, we know what Augustine thought! In commentating the Christian Psalms, he was to discover an active, occult beauty; quite the opposite of the passive beauty of numbers and laws. It makes use of these, oh yes; so that noticing them is important and delightful. But it works entirely in and through the *Beholder*. In turn, the beholder finds that he is deeply and urgently thankful to whomever has made this possible. And this desire to pour out praise in his high exultant state is pursued in the ongoing commentary and affects it in turn. Scripture opens up and seems receptive to it. The commentator finds that he is seeing all of it under some new aspect, ostensibly personal to him and yet sounding unequivocally through the whole. This was Augustine's experience again and again. And it gives his commentaries on the Psalms their peculiar quality – Which Laurence is wanting to tell us is their peculiar musical quality, and the moment, then, in which music and theology, the natural and the supernatural, come together on a point to explain each other.]

In a way that might surprise the modern musicologist, this approach of Augustine's can by turns also be unbelievably precise and exacting: producing results that would be too fine for the dragnet of science, or simply to elusive. Or again, simply too peculiar or personal in origination (but which are then shown to hold true). He marks a distinction between *singing* and *praise* on the basis of means and ends, for example.[27] Likewise, the harp and the cithara have their different symbolisms and their different uses in metaphor. Musical analogies redouble for Augustine and abound as he strains every word for its spiritual meaning. Every word of Sacred Scripture is treated in this way in order to reveal its secrets, new each time. The more mysterious the text before Augustine, the more it appears to call to him to be interpreted. Only when he can at last connect it to what it is pointing to in signification, can he reveal its secret.[28]

From the point of view of hermeneutics, this approach of Augustine's presses the difference between, again, the modern way of closing the researcher and reader to all but the historical value in the text and Augustine's way, in which the human mind is instead opened in imagination and discovers in response and in sync, a text which is in the same way open and alive. Like his friend and physician, Gennadius, Augustine will find that he is hearing and drawing to a melody, his words coming together mysteriously as he does so; and forming into their own 'melody' as he does so. Perhaps this answers the Editor's question above. Perhaps what is beautiful in music is not the appreciation and manipulation of method and form but the opportunity to follow a melody – the musical melody being the closest we can come on earth, to speech without words. Accordingly, Augustine will melt each word in order to reduce it to its true density and to allow it to flow where it will. This 'sacred game' might look like playfulness and speculation in comparison to the rigid protocol of modern scientific investigation, but in truth, the two approaches bear no comparison. Augustine is working within the world of signs and significations, in which one object, or one word, or one phrase, might stand for an infinity of meanings. This infinity of possible meanings is guaranteed and made possible by the imagination of Augustine in conjunction with the imagination of his reader. And by the sacred text itself, of course, which appears to meet Augustine, and then his reader, wherever they are. It is not by accident, then, that Augustine will reflect on numerous occasions in his commentaries, on *the reader*. In particular, Augustine wants to stress how what is written can never (in point of technical fact) be read in quite the way it was written, because always in between, will intervene the fact of interpretation – the fact of the necessary interpretative gap between writer and reader. Each privileged by a personal outlook which the other cannot share. I believe this to be one of the limits of language, but also then one of its strengths. A strength, certainly, for a writer with spiritual ambitions such as Augustine. Indeed, Augustine is well aware that given the interpretative gap which otherwise stands, it is in the nature of reading comprehension that it requires a certain partiality on the part of the reader. Good and effective writing makes an accomplice of the reader. If we set this then within the Christian and Christian-spiritual dimension, we see an opportunity to say that grace must be at work to recover the interpretative gap each time. This, certainly, is Augustine's feeling on the matter: and it is his aim when speaking of these things, to encourage his reader not to rush, and to make the space for grace to work. Often, he hopes to hit upon a direct similarity of experience: 'They will not be able to comprehend me completely unless they have tasted for themselves that of which I speak.'[29] However, sheer sympathy can go a long way in this direction and Augustine concedes that if the reader can draw close enough in their heart, to the heart of the writer, and then bring in their imagination at the critical point for the rest, they can come close – even spookily close – to sharing in the original experience of the writer. To seeing it through the writer's eyes: 'He is my friend who can be so moved to contemplate along with me.'[30] Thus we have arrived at the element of *love*, and the role of love, in the Augustinian scheme;[31] for love covers everything that we have been saying here of melody and of the necessity of partiality and sympathy between reader and writer.

Augustine gives to reason its traditional role, but at its limit, that is when it can go no further, he lets it that love must take over. Love is properly then at the centre of the Augustinian cognitive process. Love is both the point of departure and the point of arrival for the trinity of *believing – understanding – knowing*. In this scheme, the reader most definitely aims at participation and the performativity of Sacred Scripture qua text, offers the opportunity. The object of music is similar to that of the Sacred Word, in the way that the object of the orator is similar to that of the preacher and the composer. Which is to move in order to transport, to penetrate to the most intimate place where the abstraction of the word (its breaking apart into infinity possibility) becomes the real experience, and the concrete, sensible, affective experience (the experience remembered afterwards), on the part of the listener. The performed and sounded word touches off something huge and uncontrolled in the listener. When Augustine sat in church that famous time, and was moved and transported to tears, we say that he did not exit that church as he entered it. We say that he was changed by the imprinting of a memory. (Oh, the power of a memory, which changes us by walking alongside us for ever more!) And in his commentary on Psalm 30, we find a parallel, turned now into a command to the faithful as they sit and listen to the Psalm sung:

> If the Psalm prays, you pray! If it moans, you moan! If it gives thanks, you rejoice! If it hopes, you hope! If it fears, you fear! And you shall do this because everything here has been written so as to be your mirror.[32]

As he looks at himself in the mirror of the text, the reader/singer/listener learns to know himself, becoming that which is sung and is perfected.[33] The great danger otherwise in this life is that we in fact do have all the words and descriptions and theories at our command. We can document this world – and ourselves as parts of it – till kingdom come. Platonism and rationalism show this. What Augustine is trying to alert us to in his commentaries on the Psalms is that we lose sight of who we really are, and where we really might be, by doing that. The goal of the Psalmist, and now of Augustine, must be to place before us great but stark musical images, into which we may enter by *experience* – the images of the Christian, the Prophet, the Saint, the Son and the Father. Otherwise, we remain trapped in the analytical part of our minds, 'behind the glass', looking on from a respectful distance and never being *moved*. It is like Pier Paolo Pasolini lamented in his 'Letter from Benares', in which he says as much as that, *We have all the words! (Mysticism and the true heart of man has always yearned for what is beyond them, in their eradication. For words are the human 'creation'. The true Creation must in comparison look and feel like silence.)*

> Si ripete così la vecchia storia: il mondo stupendo, e orrendo e io che lo contemplo, ricco, fin troppo ricco, degli strumenti necessari a registrarlo.[34]

> [*Editor:* Yes, I believe Laurence is correct here and I believe it fully justifies the risk she has run in opening herself up to this in her reading of Augustine and in using her own heart and mind as the experimental case. *Melody* is the answer to my question why the notes go together as they do to make music that is beautiful, when it is avowedly so. And therefore melody also keeps it that music, and music's beauty, is a very special symbolism indeed and a very special mystery. For there is and can be no method

to melody's composition, yet when once a melody has been expressed, it is as though it always existed and it is as though its notes always belonged together in exactly that arrangement. This predestination is not countenanced in musical theory, which, being *theory*, has eyes only for what connects the notes (after the fact), not the notes themselves. I think this also allows us to take full and final stock of Laurence's achievement in this book. She has chosen to follow Augustine's notes literally and faithfully, not the connections between them. We are taught at school and university in the West at least, that the theory of how something goes together is superior in every respect to the thing-gone-together. Laurence shows here that it is a world apart! She has bent the ear of her heart and heard and replayed for us the melody in Augustine's commentaries on the Psalms. How different this is from stepping back and dividing through them by some or other denominator in order to measure their contribution to 'this' or 'that' discipline, will now become apparent.]

1

The Christian

In Christian thought, man is made in the image of God.[1] But this image has been discoloured by sin. Christ came to earth to 're-form man after the image of God'[2] and it is the task of man at the same time not to deform any further the divine image which he carries about within him, and which furnishes him with such basic graces as the lights of conscience; notwithstanding his fallen nature. 'The image of God is found inside us, there where the intellect is, the mind, the reason that seeks after truth; there where faith is and hope and love.'[3] Every time that man truly understands, that he truly seeks after the truth, that he believes and hopes and loves, the image of God within him is coloured anew. From this principle, eminently visible, comes a trove of hidden musical allegories and analogies of sound.

For the image is completed in its sonorous dimension, with the union of *The Word* with the word of man. The creation is a discursive act. God spoke, and the things were made.[4] He pronounced a word, and created man.[5] He did not paint, he did not imagine (he did not *theorise*!), but he spoke; and by speaking, he conferred to man *The Word*. And correspondingly, when he wishes to put his finger down on what characterizes man, Augustine passes over our linguistic faculty qua discourse, and over our spoken voice qua denoting and signifying, and comes down instead on music. Yes, to Augustine, man has been created in the sonorous image of *The Word*, so that fallen, and held here in the Earthly City, he sings and sounds in the hope of being transformed back into the resonant musical instrument he was made.

The sacrifice of song

One of the starting points in reconstructing this Augustinian image of the musical man is to pursue the theme of praise. For in praising God, man comes close to his Creator and revives the image otherwise discoloured by sin. The question of praise, joined as it is to the questions of words and song, comes to be thought of in analogy with musical instruments, and then finally, when a point and pitch of praise are reached when words and song and sound will no longer suffice, this praise is consumed in silence.

To the performative voice of God is joined – then – the performative song of man. We see in this the circularity of the speculative voice in its movement between the Divine and man. God speaks continuously through an unlimited variety of means. From the angels to the true words of men, 'It is always him who everywhere makes heard his voice, touching, encouraging, inspiring.'[6] The Divine Voice touches lovingly like the Son, loves encouragingly like the Father, inspires like the Spirit – we say that it does all of this after the manner of music, when music transforms he who follows it and hears it.

According to this theme of praise – set within a vision of divine performativity – Augustine investigates the source of song and of song's words, as well as the nature of song and of its effects. In order to be performed in the first place, the song must respect certain criteria. And so Augustine theorizes the internal and external conditions, looking at and defining the interior attitude of the singer and the external manifestations of his song.

'In cantico amantis affectio' (In song, there is the affection of one loving)

For Augustine, the song of praise amounts to the forging of a 'new alliance'. To the supreme sacrifice of the God-man, glorious in its humility, responds the sacrifice of praise that glorifies God and benefits man. The praise is the sonorous sign of the offering made in the heart.[7] Christ is given to men with the word and with the *kiss of Grace* – freely – to whom man responds by rendering Grace.[8]

The encomiastic song is therefore joined with the transforming power of the advent of Christ as the *new man* and contains within itself, therefore, a free and freely moving power. The old hymn, the old man and the Old Testament are taken over by the new hymn – Christ – by the renovated song and *The Renovator*, gifted by God to men that they might sing and know how to praise.[9] And this song acts, then, as though God had conferred to men his very power-to-act. 'We speak a hymn to our God, and this same hymn frees us.'[10] In these words, we see indicated not only the object of worship but the action of the song; plus, Augustine also makes clear in them that *invocation* is to be considered synonymous with *singing*. Namely, 'invoke by praising, sing the hymn to your God'.[11] Augustine means that the hymn of praise departs from God precisely in order to return to him (through us).

The question of the source of music of praise is theological before it is musical: the song does not have its providence in man, but is a gift of God. Recognition of the goods received from God – a motif of Augustine's thought and a gloss of 1 Cor 4, 7: 'What do you have that you did not receive?' – holds true also, then, for the new song. If all goods come from God, then man receives them for himself, for his benefit. That is to say, the song is not given because it is useful to God but because it is useful to man. Which makes it therefore that it is inseparable from *hearing*, from hearing God – a central theme of Christian and Augustinian thought. Man receives in order to give (back to God). Therefore, in order to know how to receive, he must know how to listen. On earth, man cannot be the perfect image of God; however, it is possible for him to come into accord with the Divine Will and to listen to it. By listening to it, man hears what he should sing in return.

God instils the words of the song, inspiring him who listens in silence, in *quiet*.[12] Augustine intends this to speak to composers and poets and to all artists who wish to question their creativity from the theological point of view. For example, various expressions can translate the formula: 'Praise your words in God'. Here, we are choosing to see the source of musical and poetic inspiration, according to Augustine; viz., that such words are in the artist because they are put there by God, yet are truly enough said to be *from* the artist insofar as the artist has duly accepted their provenance: 'They have reached me, they have become mine'.[13]

On the way to all of this, Augustine distinguishes between the (mere) physical act of listening and listening-with-understanding, his idea being that the latter incorporates the enjoyment of what is being heard plus intuitions as to what is intended in the words. He distinguishes, then, between the roles of sense and intellect in listening (to the Divine Will) and in the words eventually sung (in response). Verses 6 and 7 of Psalm 25 – 'I wash my hands in innocence, and go about your altar, O Lord, proclaiming aloud your praise and telling of all your wonderful deeds.' – give Augustine the opportunity to develop these various concepts inherent in the song of praise. The voice of praise is first apprehended by the interior ear that divines its intention: 'He who has ears, let him hear.'[14] Then, in order to sing it out properly and well as his own song, man has first to listen to the voice, and then to listen to it again with understanding. Only then can he put it into the song it deserves and calls for. Many hear but they do not, in this sense, listen. They have ears, but they remain dead to the truth. Listening, in its full Augustinian meaning, means comprehension.[15]

'To listen is to comprehend interiorly;'[16] it is to open oneself to the interiority of being and intention. Intelligent listening plus the heart that welcomes the sensible sound or the Divine Voice is the point of departure of praise. He who does not have the capacity for this may neither pronounce on it nor sing of it. From him, the truth of the word flees to another (where it can be received); as does the Divine Word then flee, as well as all that was Divine in the Word (nothing remains!). In order not to tarnish the image of God, Augustine is calling on men to work with the intelligence that differentiates them from the beasts, or from the non-rational creation. 'Do not be like the horse or the mule, which have no understanding.'[17] Every time that man listens by his interior ear to the words spoken, the image is rendered clear again.

This interior comprehension, being vital to the singing of the Psalms and indeed having stimulated them originally, should not and cannot be severed from the love that realizes the law and which has been left in heredity to all men. Commentating on the closing of Psalm 71 – 'This concludes the prayers of David son of Jesse' – Augustine talks of song and of affection and delineates a question essential to music, and which has worked its way across the history of music. Namely, the indissociability of word and sentiment in a saying or phrase that, in music, can never (otherwise) betray the affective content enclosed in the words (alone). That is to say, the role of the listener, and how music must calculate on it and figure on it; and the role of partiality and inclination and love in that listener. Looking at Psalm 71, Augustine spies an opportunity to latch on for his readers to this organic relationship between words and music, as it occurs in the definition – in his definition – of hymns. Thus, hymns are, 'praises to God united in song.' If one of these components is missing – 'if there is praise, but not in honour of God, or if there is praise in honour of God but it is not sung' – we are not speaking of a hymn. Augustine is not the only one to define the hymn in its relationship to song, but he goes furthest in underlining the affective element contained within the song and carried by it: 'whoever sings their praise not only then praises but praises with joy'. The song is praise's joyous expression and contains always, also – within the bosom of that joy – the love with which it was sung: 'whoever sings in praise, not only sings but loves him of whom he sings' (*in cantico amantis affectio*).[18] In this way, as will be done again, for example, in his commentary on Psalm 76, Augustine weaves together and inseparably singing, joy and love. Whoever sings, loves. And whoever loves, cannot but be joyful.[19]

These properties of the song of praise and the hymn are turned immediately by Augustine, to the 'new song': 'The song is a thing of joy, and if we consider the matter with due diligence, also a thing of love. Therefore, whosoever knows how to love the new life, knows how to sing the new song.'[20] The joy that is synonymous with love is united in the coupling, *to sing/to love*: the song is the manifestation of joy and therefore of love, and because love is, like music, totally involving, the new man sings with all his person: 'they sing with their voices and their hearts; they sing with their lips and with their mores.'[21] The new musical man sings out the object of his love. He does not want to sing of anything else and, filled with joy, he cannot stop.[22] He sings what he loves, and therefore he is himself transformed in song. 'The praise supplies the song as well as the singer': there, resplendent, is the image of that which, though invisible, is loved – the love itself.

> So ... a man falls in love with a beautiful woman. We do not deny that the motive in this case is the beauty of her body. Yet that which is sought by the man, and by the woman if she responds, is the exchange proper to love ... She looks at him, he looks at her, but outside of this (exchange), love itself is not seen.[23]

Love is seen only in the form of lovers who look at each other, and looking at each other, sing the new song, transforming themselves in the singing of its praise, and reformed to the image of the source of every love: 'Do you wish to send up praises to God? Then be the praise ... Do you wish to know where God might be? Then look to yourselves!'[24] In this way, the deification of man takes place through his transformation in sung praise.

In addition to listening (to the Divine Will) as the condition of song, we have added most emphatically, then, love. As we have seen, that the song might be real, there too must be love: and so the song understood as the effect of love becomes confounded with the *affect* of love conveyed by the song. Love, the first theological virtue, is absolutely necessary for sacred song, ecclesial or private, exterior or interior, during the liturgy or in front of the altar of the heart. This first virtue and only law of the new man sustains and animates him as he sings; and while he sings, it conveys the love that is invading him. Thus is closed the *affective circle of music*. With love now placed at the opening and at the end of music, music becomes an act of contemplation. And this, of course, was how Thomas Aquinas was to describe contemplation. Like a circle, it is born from love and returns therein to be reborn again only more enriched by that same love.[25] And the middle term that unites contemplation and music is *delight*: the delight that in music carries one up to contemplation, and in contemplation, closes in on the object of love.

For Augustine, song becomes the moment in which joyous love is manifested. It contains and declares the affection of those who love. 'In song there is the affection of the lover,'[26] writes Augustine, expressing in this short phrase, in a manner emblematic, the nexus between love and sacred song. The theme will recur in various discourses of his: one cannot sing if one is not first animated by love. And this absolute condition – this impossibility of song without love – Augustine will encourage us to think of both allegorically and practically.

'Cantate cordibus' (To sing from the heart): From the hymns of David to spiritual praise

To better understand this impossibility of singing without love, it will be convenient for us to return to the theological exposition of Psalm 72. There, we read that David's population ceased to sing their hymns after they saw the material riches coming to those who did not so bother to sing to God. They watched as the wicked were 'rewarded' with good things and their faith faltered. It became difficult to praise a God whom they suspected now to be unjust. From this, Augustine draws out the fact that the song is a signification of love, tied tightly to the faith of the lover.[27] If one does not, or cannot believe in whom one loves, or does not or cannot love the one in whom one believes, any song forthcoming can exhibit only an external *formalism*. That is, it can bear only the mechanical form of a song, but empty of heart. Here, Augustine has brought in the personal responsibility pertaining to the faithful, but also to the Church in her song. He has underlined that the sacred song can never be something merely practised or 'carried out', an empty vestige of sound, but rather must be filled with affection in order to meet its very condition of being as a sign.

In this way, Augustine makes clear what for him are the conditions of the sacred song in terms of listening and affect. The sacred song thus defined should also be thought of in terms of its relationship to the new law. The kingdom of King David stood for the time when the New Testament was concealed in the Old Testament, as Christ was amongst the patriarchs. The first was, then, already the second, as the fruit grows from the root. The time of the patriarchs gave place to Christ, son and saviour of David. And the carnal sacrifices of man to God became spiritual praises. And the hymns of David ceased, too.[28] We say that the time of Christ was the advent of the silent spiritual song which magnifies in a manner entirely new, the joyous affection in the law of love.

In silent song – the interior sacrifice of praise – a perfume is exhaled that gladdens God.[29] Not by chance does Augustine make use of an olfactory analogy. For the perfume, in its evanescence, penetrates the body, like the sung sacrifice that now takes place in the most intimate place of one's being. The silent song – the very highest form of praise – puts song into an altogether new dimension. Listening and affect now come together and take place in the conscience – the intimate place par excellence, where is heard the very voice of truth, the voice of God and of Being. By this means, Augustine points to another basic condition of the new song. Which being that in order to sing, one must have recourse to one's true interiority: '"In me, O God, are the votive offerings that you will render." Otherwise I feared that you would impose on me something from outside of me.'[30] But God does not impose anything that is outside of man. The new song of praise draws from the conscience because the conscience is the one part of man that no one can destroy (from the outside). A song drawn from such a place is an image of the songs of the angels. A song always present because it is present in most intimate interiority. Inviolable. Thus, Augustine invites introspection: 'I will re-enter into myself, in order to find there what I can offer up to you. I will re-enter into myself, and in myself I will find the sacrifice of praise. My conscience will be my altar.'[31] The temple of God is the heart of man. His altar is man's conscience. And from these sacred places floats the song of praise.

By this point, the image has united with the song. The image of the face of the Divine is seen in the song of joy which in turn transfigures the face of existence. This joy does manifest itself exteriorly, but also is said in silence.[32] In this way, the exterior song manifests the inaudible song of the heart. The exterior song is only the corporeal aspect, but it is a necessary aspect. 'There comes to lips that which is held interiorly.'[33] But the full truth of the matter outruns the mere description of it and must wait upon one who has at last had this full same experience themselves, and tasted of it.[34]

By trying to enter into the labyrinth of the conscience, and, on the themes of intimacy and listening, by trying to investigate praise in parallel with proper (just) wordage and affection, Augustine passes between the discourses of philosophy, theology and anthropology and shows how altogether, they go into defining the song of praise. This song departs from silence and returns to silence in the absolute purity of its spiritual expression. It departs from the listener (of the Divine Will) in order to be listened to by others in turn. It is born in the affection which contains it; it manifests that affection and reinforces it; and then it returns that affection back to itself, stronger than before. In this way, this idea, according to which the song encases the affections and strongholds them, can be seen to integrate classical musical theory's concept of *ethos* with the theological concept of *faith*.

We say that silence, listening, affection, love and conscience come together to be thought of at once musically and theologically. The silence before the song is the silence of the disciple who waits upon a voice far greater than his, and the hearer of his song in turn is a believer who seeks inspiration from a voice that has become superior and intimate, superior *because* intimate.

'I will turn my ear': Listening to music intelligently

'I will turn my ear to a proverb; with the harp I will expound my riddle' (Ps 48, 5). Who are these who, meditating in the heart, speak with intelligence? Who are these who speak not only superficially, with the lips, but can possess the most intimate place of a man? Who are these who listen in order to speak in this way? Because many there who speak without listening. And who are these? They are those who do not do as they say, like those Pharisees of whom the Saviour said that they sit on the Chair of Moses ... That is, they do not listen to the things they are saying. By contrast, those who do out what they say, listen to what they say: and therefore we say that they speak fruitfully because they have listened. Those who speak and do not listen, may (at times) profit others, but they do not profit themselves. However, in order to indicate those who do want to listen and speak – those whom we wish to draw attention to here – before the Psalmist said the following: 'with the harp I will expound my riddle' (signifying thereby that he was speaking in corporeal terms, insofar as we are to understand that the soul is served by the body as the harpist is served by the harp), he said: 'I will turn my ear to a proverb'. That is, before speaking to you by means of his body, before playing for you his harp, he means you to know that he will 'turn [his] ear to a proverb', namely, that he will listen for that which he will then say.[35]

This relentless focus of Augustine on listening is accounted for by the importance he places on universal justice. Listening, the basic principle of Christian faith *ex auditu*, as well as of the inspired word and of wise music, is in fact also the criterion that is going to divide men on the *Last Day*.[36] To the one side, will go those who listen only in distraction, to distracting things – who choose to close up their ears on the threshold of revelation and possess what they can. To the other side, will go those who listen with intelligence and keenly – who choose to incline themselves and to open their minds: 'He who has ears, let him hear.'[37] We see then that Augustine has made it that that which we listen to intelligently, with a view to our salvation, is to be explained by the musical paradigm of the image of the psalter, or the harp; for him now the instrument that symbolizes the understanding of the law. This is how Augustine commentates verse 5 of Psalm 48, 'I will turn my ear to a proverb; with the harp I will expound my riddle.'

Turning is the prelude to explanation, listening to expounding. Whosoever has listened with an open heart – ear bowed in humble attention – may now stretch out the words in exposition on the stringed instrument. Intelligence is properly developed in this meditation in the heart: the heart does not err and its ear always hears.[38] 'I have heard with the ear of the heart. Now, I have no motive for doubt.'[39] That which has been recorded in the ear of the heart cannot be misunderstood: it makes for intimate certainties which quite simply are over and above rational doubt. And in music, this intelligence of the heart finds its natural and perfect outlet as it speaks upon the harp: 'not only speaking superficially, with the lips, but possessing the most intimate place of a man'.[40] This intimate place is inhabited by that which the heart hears and understands, and which it plays out upon the instrument of music. As Nicholas of Cusa will observe, 'The harp is the work of intelligence.'[41] That is to say, it represents the most intimate comprehension of things in the union of mind and heart, and of word and affection. This instrument of David allegorizes the interior law of the new man: the new man who listens and who speaks on the harp, and who unites then listening, thought, word and action. The ideal of justice – namely, that whosoever listens in the heart possesses what is heard – coincides perfectly with musical practice.

The general debate in musical theory on the union of music and poetry – on the instrumental sound with the words – has its allegorical reflection in the field of theology. The word, on its own, must remain on the surface of the lips, and the musical sound, on its own, cannot convey any semantic content. 'To play the word on the harp', however, allows it to penetrate the most intimate place of the listener, *mediated* by sound and *meditated* upon by the heart. The listener is turned (in anticipation) to the proverb, to the word, to the harp, even before a single note has been sounded. Likewise, the word sung upon the harp cannot but be followed by the listener in a way neither sterile nor servile, but advantageous.[42] 'What produces this listening?'[43] Quite simply, the sheer joy of hearing something securely and the possibility of speaking it out. It is always – like this – a listening in order to say, to sing, to play. Once again, we encounter the central theme of the primacy of listening, which is the same for the song of praise: 'that they might fruitfully speak because they listened'.[44] If this is the plain truth, then a kaleidoscope of concepts do nonetheless come together to make up the theme of musical listening.

If God speaks in order that man might sing his praises, in Augustine's commentary on Psalm 48, the soul speaks in order that the body might express it. The word of the soul stands in the same relation to the human body as God does to the word of man. By this means, Augustine proposes yet another level of interpretation for that verse of Psalm 48 that goes, 'with the harp I will expound my riddle'. To 'expound the riddle (word) upon the harp' signifies to speak corporeally: for the harp is the musical image of the words pronounced. Again, listening always comes first. God speaks, and man listens. Really, the soul listens, and then speaks in the (interior of the) man as sounded-out words. To these, the man bows his ear in reverence before expounding them upon his harp.

'Before speaking to you by means of his body, before playing for you his harp, he means you to know that he will "turn [his] ear to a proverb", namely, that he will listen for that which he will then say.'[45] He listens in his heart, the place of truth, and he listens intelligently, in order to play the harp and to say according to the law of love that which he must say – not to all, but to some; or even perhaps to just a few. Perhaps, even, to one person alone! – *That which I must say to you*. This is why Christ taught in parables: in order to secure that only those who should comprehend will comprehend and can comprehend. 'He who has ears, let him hear.'[46] Not by chance has this biblical injunction been dear to composers of cryptic music down the ages!

Yes, Augustine is introducing us here to the somewhat disconcerting idea (disconcerting to the modern Zeit, at least) of a word kept back – or reserved – for the select few; and likewise, a music kept back. Yes, there are words that are so sweet and sacred that they speak in secret and hide their sense in profundity – they do not ask to be comprehended by all. This hiddenness is the veil of allegory, of the parable, of the enigma, of the sacred word revealed in intimacy. According to Augustine, this nature of the parable is what Paul is talking about when he makes his distinction between future and present vision – now, we see as in a mirror, enigmatically.[47] On this scheme, the harp accords with the mirror and hearing with the look into it. The analogy between the look in the mirror – we cannot see the Divine reality but mediated through creation – and the harp is explained by the corporality which they have in common. Sensible vision is in this way equivalent to the soul as it expresses itself through the body, and to the harpist as he expresses himself on his instrument.

Sound is the mediator between the soul that speaks in silence and *the other*, who, without the sound, would more often than not struggle to 'hear' that soul's thoughts. Which is the same thing as to say that it is the listening to the parable, to the word in the mirror, mediated and enigmatic, indirect and not directly comprehensible, that makes its enunciation (and enumeration) in sound possible. In this way, intelligence is preserved: 'The enigma is an obscure parable that is difficult to hear. As far as a man can purify his heart, and turn his intelligence to interior things ... he may yet see only but a part (due to the corruption of his flesh).'[48] Whether we are talking of the Divine mind visible only in the mirror of creation, or the parable in the sacred text, or the secret word in the interior of some *other*: in all these cases, we cannot ever talk of arriving at full comprehension. The heart of man is a mystery even to himself who never does penetrate its depths. And even when he does manage to gaze interiorly with intelligence, he sees only in part.

Music plays a privileged part in the cryptic spectacle of the parable. If it were all totally transparent, as it will be at the final trumpet, there would of course be no need of mediation by the harp. One listens in order to speak, and one speaks upon the harp, so that intelligence might manifest itself in the corporeality of the sound. This wise musical listening involves all of the musical man: the soul and the body, the intellect and the heart. The sonorous mediation is necessary: for insofar as we are human, we have need of the senses, of sounds – of the intelligent sound that unites the soul to the body in the body of the musical instrument.

Silence, listening, affection, love and conscience all define the musical man who perfects himself by knowing them. But at the same time, they define also the limits of song. The distance between the human word and the Divine reality, and therefore the limits of articulated language (also then of music) when it comes to speaking of God, is a subject of longstanding importance in Christian thought. Just think of negative theology and of the reflections on language from the Oriental and Western mystics. And Augustine, too, of course, will devote famous attention to the subject. Not least in his commentary on Psalm 26, in which he will develop his thoughts in a musical key.

'Nullis verbis' (With no words)

The human song and its limits are to be considered, in the Augustinian framework, according to the images Augustine develops of the Ineffable Modulator of the *song of the universe*. The Creator not only shapes, but orders everything; and the musical image put forward by Augustine to represent the mutable beauty of this universal order is that of a song, conducted by the Divine hand.

> For the change suitable to the present age has been enjoined by God, who knows infinitely better than man what is fitting for every age, and who is, whether He give or add, abolish or curtail, increase or diminish, the unchangeable Governor as He is the unchangeable Creator of mutable things, ordering all events in His providence until the beauty of the completed course of time, the component parts of which are the dispensations adapted to each successive age, shall be finished, like the grand melody of some ineffably wise master of song, and those pass into the eternal immediate contemplation of God who here, though it is a time of faith, not of sight, are acceptably worshipping Him.[49]

The Wisdom of the Creator who gives and takes according the needs of his creatures forms therefore the *Great Song* – the song of the universe, always incomprehensible in toto to the creature bound up in it, who can see it only part in part. This song of the universe, in its sighs and its swells, in its pauses and in its silences, is the work of a Composer-God. God did not choose to paint the universe in painting's correspondingly static mode. The Ineffable Modulator is always presenting himself newly in being, modulating his presence and his love by reshaping being according to his needs. At the heart of this song, he takes but also offers – contemporaneously – his gifts.

The invitation to gaze upon and to praise this spectacle of created reality in all its harmonious variety comes hand-in-hand with the invitation to consider oneself also such a spectacle: 'You who wish to look, be ye also the spectacle.'⁵⁰ Man, both actor and spectator, musician and listener, participates in the spectacle of creation and sees the other created things in the perfection impressed upon them by the Highest Director. In this vision, his role becomes to sing the ordinate praise (back) to the Creator.

Creation is, then, in the Augustinian vision, a sonorous spectacle: all of it resounds in voices, speaking and singing of its Divine origin. From mere, unarticulated sound to full-on song, everything gives testimony of the imprint of the Highest Modulator, while man echoes all of this in his song of praise to God.

> If it were possible for your spirit to make the tour of all Creation, then everywhere to you would cry everything: *God made me.* Everything would sing to you by the arts of praise of its Artificer. The more that you toured, the more would this praise assail you. Observe the skies, what great works they are of God. Observe the earth: God has decided the numbers of seeds, the variety of germinations, the multitudes of animals. Make again your tour from the heavens down to the earth and do not leave out anything: everywhere each thing will speak to you of the Creator [resound in praise of the Creator], in such manner as every creature according to its species, contributes its voice to the hymn of praise to God.⁵¹

Reality gives testimony by *resounding*, and the creatures give up the voice appropriate to their species. Thus, is the Creator praised. And yet, we have to notice that for all of this resounding and for all these voices, the praise cannot be such as that it expresses exactly and explicitly what it praises. This is the question, or the principle of, *worthiness* – of the necessity of praise to drop short of the majesty of the Creator. 'Who can worthily praise the heavens, the earth, the sea and all the creatures in it?'⁵² This in fact introduces us to one of the conditions of praise, if we think about it. Otherwise, praise would at some point have completed its round of work, and cease. But it goes on, because it is insufficient (and in being insufficient, it marks the category of difference between Creator and created). 'Who can worthily praise the angels?'⁵³ Augustine's point is that no one can speak worthily for the same reason that no one can speak worthily of the rhythmic impulse that runs through the human body: 'who can praise worthily the vital momentum that is in us?'[54] This rhythmic energy ('By the measure of rhythm we speak of a determined capacity for movement.'[55]) is the part of man that suspends him between the earth and the angels. It animates both his material and immaterial parts. That is, his memory (the 'dynamism of the soul' that records his sensible experiences[56]) and his intelligence. The vital momentum is the active principle, the movement, the awakening, the embrace and the comprehension: 'It vivifies the body, moves the members, awakens the senses, embraces many things in the memory, and discerns many things in intelligence.'[57] The reawakening of the senses and the embracing by memory and the comprehension following upon it are ineffable. The three *perfections of existence*, namely, the beauty of things visible, the angels and the fluid vitality of being, are such that there is no one on earth who can speak properly or worthily of them.

To praise the Divine art in creation as it should be praised, man simply does not have the expressions or language at his disposal; less still to praise the Divine Artificer Himself! No mere word is able to speak of the Creator, or even to think on him – as Pseudo-Dionysius warned: 'In no wise should you dare to say or think anything concerning super-substantial Divinity.'[58] This Divinity must not, so to speak, become thus a victim of the sheer joy, or ebullience, in human nature; or for that matter, in its own Divine nature. The proper way is for the atoning host to carry about him a joy which he acknowledges is uncontainable, yet which he never attempts to enclose fully in words or voice.[59] *The Joy* is experienced as a joy that runs on without being marshalled or understood or translated. This is why, when the Psalmist comes to speaking of unspeakable things, he both speaks and does not speak them. And in his reading of the Psalm, Augustine for his part marks this, and using intuition, passes beyond the visible language of the words to come on to that of which they truly are the testimony. 'I catch glimpse of the great thing you promise. You want to say it, but you do not. Is it because you cannot, or because if you did, we would not comprehend?'[60] The situation of Paul – who heard Divine words which could not then be communicated to men at large – becomes here the impossibility of saying and thinking that which is announced but perceived only in part (as the full-score Divinity of the universe is perceived only in part). In the perception of the ineffable, one leaves behind the human word and enters – or part enters – into the Divine, which is untouched by human language. 'If ever you come on to that ineffable happiness, your human mind has failed you and become divine.'[61] This divinization of man happens every time that he comes on to unspeakable joy.

'I expressed myself as I could, and as I saw, but I could not express what I saw.'[62] This inexpressibility is unavoidable, because it is simply the case that whatever is over and above reason is over and above logic and language too! This is why Augustine must refer to the divinization of the human mind, otherwise it would of itself – by its very rationality – block all possibility of going beyond it to higher things. This 'fading away of the man in the man' leaves space for the Divine in man. 'In no wise can we express the beauty of the Divine sweetness.'[63] And yet, the song does turn precisely to the expression of praise: 'In an ineffable way I praised the Lord. "I will sing and make psalms to the Lord" (*Cantabo et psallam Domino*). We will be sure. Surely we shall sing and surely we shall tell.'[64] 'I will sing to the Lord … And I will tell of the name of the Lord.'[65] We see here that the distinction between the song and the hymn, as elsewhere in Augustine, is the distinction between interiority and exteriority: in the sense that, one sings in one's heart and one praises in one's works.[66] With thought, goes song; with works, praise. This distinction shows all over again that the song is a thing eminently intimate and the highest expression of thought. But another characteristic of song shows itself in Augustine's commentary above in the use of the future tense: *I will sing*. While ineffable praise comes to be expressed in the past tense, songs and hymns are expressed in the future tense. The song is reserved for the future because it is the expression of a praise that is for now, impossible. The musical man sings in his heart and praises in his works, but from the eschatological perspective, he will only sing fully when he has taken reception of the perfect joy that awaits him.

In the contemplation of sweetness, musical praise is consumed by silence. This silence is no less than a speech that is over and above words. It is, as it were, a word returned to the heart of the musical man and to his mind-made-Divine in accordance with its true interior listening of inexpressible affection. When all that possibly could have been said, is said – through voice, through song, through all the senses in every which way – you arrive at the essence of what cannot be said. Not even in song can this ineffable be enunciated. All that remains is silent praise. The maximum praise.

Man as chitara and harp

The song of the conscience is united to the music of the musical instruments, therewith to complete the sonorous image. The image of the musical man integrates the corporeal and incorporeal dimensions: when the body, soul and spirit of man are well tempered on the chitara, then he can sing.[67]

Psalm 32, which calls for the Lord to be celebrated on the chitara and the ten-stringed harp with a new song, is, on Augustine's reckoning, the point at which the praise returned to God by man is accomplished in the man at last transformed into the appropriate musical instrument.[68] When we sing and meditate upon this Psalm, says Augustine, we must bring into our minds the musical instruments employed in the theatre (*organa theatrica*). The chitara and the harp mentioned in the Psalm refer to man. The identification of these musical instruments with man expresses the idea that the praise most perfect would be the same thing as the human being most perfect – in just the same way that the principal miracle of God was to make man himself.[69] In this context, the praise does not refer to any kind of Church song, but to the musical man, understood now to be chitara and harp and song together – each declined by Augustine, one-by-one, in unfolding paragraphs of his commentary. A veritable organological journey!

Organological symbolism

'What does it mean to praise upon the chitara and to praise upon the harp?'[70] The sacred text would not have used these different words unless it intended to signify different things: beginning with this principle, Augustine investigates the similarities and dissimilarities between the instruments in order to trace out the allegorical sense.

> Between these two musical instruments, the harp and the chitara, there is this difference: that the harp has in its upper regions a concave in the wood, thanks to which the strings give their sound. The strings are plucked down below, but sound above. In the chitara, on the other hand, the concave part is down below. For this difference we say that the harp pertains to the Heavens and the chitara to the earth.[71]

This principal distinction between the chitara and the harp – as expressed in various of Augustine's commentaries on the Psalms – is between the relative positions of the sound boxes in the instruments. Without these sound boxes, the strings would not resonate. The strings are set in the wood and plucked with the plectrum. We repeat after Augustine, on the chitara, the Lord is praised. On the harp, he is psalmed.

For their corporeality and materiality, both musical instruments allegorize action. For one plays them by the hand, the organ of work: 'Both are taken in the hand and plucked by the hand, therefore both are an image of our earthly works.'[72] The analogy between playing and working will be interpreted differently in different commentaries and the instruments will become, thus, polysemic symbols. The song will remain the image of spiritual reality while the musical instruments, made of wood or skin, will represent the corporeal. But if both instruments allegorize the work of man, each of them represents a different aspect of that work. The chitara, with its sound box below, represents the work of man in tribulation, in anxiousness, when he is expressing his fears, when he is calling out, when he is praising in amidst days of sadness, when he is conscience of his mortal condition. The harp, on the other hand, with its sound box on high, represents man stretching for the sky, as he acts according to the commandments given from on high and in the hope of the life-eternal. We will now see in detail how Augustine develops in his commentaries on Psalms 32, 42 and 91, the metaphor of the musical man transformed in song, chitara and harp.

We suffer and we play upon the chitara

> Sing softly on the chitara, keeping faith in your God. Pluck the strings of your heart and it will say, as the chitara says as it miraculously resonates in its lower part: 'The Lord gave and the Lord has taken away; may the name of the Lord be praised.'[73]

In this earthly life, the Christian must praise God in all times, happy and unhappy. In times of health and sickness. In times of peace and disturbance. When God corrects and when he consoles.[74] To play on the Chitara is man's way of thanking God for all which, in adversity and prosperity, he brings. 'Where do you imagine to assent to him who is everywhere present? Just play to him on your chitara!'[75] In abundance and privation, 'pluck the chitara in peace'.[76] With his faith in the presence of God in all times and in all things, man intones in peace upon the musical instrument. In its pacific thanks, the instrument allegorizes also the heart: 'Sing softly on the chitara, keeping faith in your God. Pluck the strings of your heart.' Praise and thankfulness in times of happiness and sorrow are consummated on these strings of the heart, which is an analogy that one will find employed well into the Renaissance, in the writings of men of letters as well as musical theorists. The chitara transformed in the human heart introduces us also, already, to the theme of our final chapter, though in the context there of silent song, shaped by Divine sound.

The chitara symbolizes, then, the earthly life with its happy and unhappy times. However, in the same way that man must learn from Christ to see the Divine things in the things earthly, so too must we not limit ourselves to thinking of the earthly life as inferior, lest in our mortal conscience we become overly sad and overcome. 'Why are you downcast, O my soul? Why so disturbed within me?'[77]

> There is to be a distinction made between our works, when they are upon the harp, when on the chitara: both however are acceptable to God, and grateful to His ear. When we do according to God's Commandments, obeying His commands and hearkening to Him, that we may fulfil His injunctions, when we are active and not passive (in response to his Voice), it is the harp that is playing. For so also do the Angels: for they have nothing to suffer. But when we suffer anything of tribulation, of trials, of offenses on this earth (as we suffer only from the inferior part of ourselves; in other words, from the fact that we are mortal, that we owe somewhat of tribulation to our original cause, and also from the fact of our suffering much from those who are not above); this is the chitara. For there rises a sweet strain from that part of us which is below: we suffer, and we sing, or shall I rather say we sing and we strike the chitara.[78]

When we act freely and obligingly, without sufferance, we work according to the Divine law, in the image of the angels. This causes us to notice that the two musical instruments – the harp and chitara –

are qualified by Augustine by the adjective 'good' if, and only if their music is produced in this free and obliging and frankly then brave way. 'Both of them are good, provided that he who plays them knows how to play the harp or knows how [and when] to play the chitara.'[79] The instruments are distinguished by the relative positions of their sound boxes, yet both make an equally sweet sound. In the passage just cited above, God's pleasure in listening to the man of music is of central importance. This qualitative dimension of sound, and the pleasure it gives to God, leads us to recognize a high value for such human works: whether made upon the harp or the chitara, 'they are pleasing to God, and sweet in their hearing.'[80] This musical and sonorous quality – this sweet sound – and how this sweetness allows us to envisage a Christian God who is pleased by the sweetness in the Universe, and who, it seems, 'hears it', in some almost human way (as we might), is a corridor to the heart of Augustine's thought and its distinctiveness. Man, musical man, the man of music, gathers up within himself the whole of creation and crowns it with his special gift and purpose as the rational creature: namely, to use his consciousness to be its consciousness, so that in him, in his music to God, it might speak with him its thankfulness to its Creator:

> In each human being all creation is present – not taken all together, that is, Heaven and earth and all the things in them, but taken in a generic sense. In each human being there is, for a start, a rational creation, which we have proved or believe that the angels possess. There is also, if I may use that term, sensual creation, which even the other animals do not lack. After all, do they not use the senses and sensual movements to seek what is useful and to avoid the opposite? And there is vital creation without sensation, such as can be found in trees. In us bodily growth comes about without our being aware of it, and hairs have no awareness, even when they are cut, and still they grow. And this is how we witness to this vital creation. Bodily creation is even more obviously apparent in us. Though the body has been made and formed from earth, it contains some particles of all the elements of this bodily world for a balanced state of health … Thus there is no kind of creature that we cannot recognize in a human being: and in that sense all of creation groans and suffers pain in us, awaiting the resurrection of the sons of God [See Rom. 8.22-23].[81]

The identification of the just works of man with a musical sound always sweet to God's ears is indeed a critical theologico-musical nexus in Augustinian thought. The works upon the harp are those actions which fulfil direct commandments spoken from on high. The man who conforms to them in obedience makes a sweet sound, as that which resonates in the sound box placed high. When, however, man works in consciousness of his fallenness and inferiority, of his sinfulness, his sound resonates within his mortal sound box placed low. Yet, as we have gone to some lengths to notice, this sound of suffering is also a sweet music. This seeming paradox of the sweetness of tribulation we recognize at once as a classic Christian theme. Yet a paradox it still can be. Here, however, through music, Augustine is able to explain it; and perhaps to explain it best. The sounds that come from below, from the lower sound box, *cannot but still be sweet because they are musical*. Augustine's point requires some concentration on our part because it is so obvious, and because it calls our bluff. Augustine is effectively countering the moral or ethical argument against the beauty of sadness (because a moral or ethical argument is what it is; it after all being the argument that it is unfair that God makes men to suffer) with the truth already admitted and expressed in art in general and most famously of all then in music, which is that sadness makes for beautiful sound. No one who has heard and been moved by sadness in music can deny this. Thus the peculiarity of the Christian message finds its ally and amplification in the working of music. Or in the event of sound. Or the *sound-event*. For we see now that it is words and their meanings that create the paradox of a good God who visits tribulation upon man. Otherwise, at the (wordless) level of sound, there is and can be no paradox, because sound can, and can only, be the true expression of the unshakeable goodness of creation (from the eternal point of view). Accordingly, in his commentary on Psalm 32, Augustine will talk of how the human aspiration to God is affirmed under blows of woe as the trumpet – as the bell of the trumpet – is made ductile and resonant under the blows of the hammer.[82] Thanks to all of this musical analogy, we are led deep into the Christian mystery of 'joy in tribulation'.

The position of the sound box in the lower part of the instrument indicates that we are dealing with earthly, fallen things, yet the undeniable sweetness of the sound produced indicates that we are hearing the eternal and omnipresent Divine Wisdom that clearly then exercises its Divinity and sweetness in all things, heavenly and earthly. This Wisdom stretches from one extremity of created reality to the other, from the angels to the animals, ordering all of it beautifully, drawing from the musical instrument the sweet sounds of its melodies – up from that sound box below, whence comes art's soaring alternative to the monochrome demands of logic, and logic's historical, temporal determinacy.

Musical sound speaks to man in the real here and now. Its sweetness invites him to consider human things from the Divine point of view, and to see their earthly beauty as a reflection of the Divine Wisdom. By this means Augustine passes from the description of musical instruments to the qualities and portents of the sounds and makes of the whole a sonorous paradigm which then he integrates into his theological reflections. As we did note quite carefully in the beginning of this volume, the use of musical sound as an analogy of Divine Wisdom in the Grand Design was as old at least as Plato. Augustine inherited it, but added to its happy thrill (the happy thrill of numbers and pure number theory!) his specific and special interpretation of Christian tribulation and the praise that pours up to God because of it and notwithstanding. In this way, Augustine united himself, and unites himself, to all art and all artists who draw their truth and beauty from sadness and suffering. Plus he offers us a large, Christian reason for the phenomenon of it. (Which perhaps does stand in need of explanation otherwise, if we think about it.)

The suffering expressed on the chitara is referred by Augustine to other theological notions, which also then become rendered musical. In particular, grace, patience, hope and glory. 'Because he could not be without tribulations, he offered to God his patience. "I will praise you with the chitara, O God, my God."'[83] In the Augustinian theory of musical affections, human tribulations are made sweet by the grace of God and also because by them, there comes the opportunity to exercise the virtue of hope. Not just the joy but the glory of tribulation is explained by Augustine in this way, taking Saint Paul as his model: 'The strings resonated from above' when the Apostle was preaching of the Saviour; 'from below on the chitara' when he was declaring that 'we glory in tribulations'.[84] The Christian finds true glory in tribulation because it tries the patience that sustains hope. True virtue is born thus in trial, so that he who fails not in the test is the one we say who knows how to play upon the chitara. He who falls, however, and is invaded with desperation, 'breaks the chitara'.[85]

Again, in this theologico-musical metaphor of Augustine's, he who breaks the chitara is he who, afflicted with desperation, has abandoned all hope and who will not – who cannot – any longer offer up praise in tribulation. It is the affect that unites the musical and human dimensions. That is to say, it is insofar as man is afflicted, that he plays the chitara. Without this affliction and its affect, there would be no musical act. And yet when he takes up the musical instrument in this extreme consciousness of his mortality, and plays it appropriately, it is nonetheless a sweet sound that emerges.[86] For the affection in the sound is a function of the sentiment of the musician in (determined) praise in conjunction with the effect produced upon the Divine ear.

In this way, the Christian mystery is confounded with the musical mystery, so that to the glory in suffering responds the sweetness of sad sound. That glory can be hidden within the bosom of suffering, and that tribulation can issue in sweetness, finds its counterpart in the incomprehensibility to this day, of sweet-sounding-sadness. In this particular theme, the speculations and the theologico-musical metaphors find their truth in the proofs of sensible experience. We say that the Passion remains as mysterious to us today as that sweet-sounding-sadness.

For Augustine, as we have seen, one must be animated by affection in order to sing; and rest assured that Augustine does not say this merely formally. No, he really means that the musician without love in his heart, *cannot sing*! The impossibility of singing without the affection of love finds its counterpart in Augustine's commentary on Psalm 42: whoever is not sad cannot praise by playing and singing upon the chitara. Not even in this scenario are we speaking of merely an 'abstract, or academic, impossibility'. If the musician is the image of faithfulness, then the entire person of him must be involved in the musical act as in the act of faith.

In this way, we get taken further in to the association between the biblical passage – 'Why are you downcast, O my soul'[87] – and music. The interrogation of man which takes place in Augustine's commentary on Psalm 42 is really a musical dialogue between man and himself. That is to say, man is not speaking in echo – and in response to – the words of the dying Christ (see below), but rather his own soul is speaking with his own body:

> Again he asks his soul, in order that it might pick up the sound that is echoing from that resonant wood in the (sound box) below: 'Why are you downcast, O my soul? Why so disturbed within me?'[88]

The sound emitted in suffering must be heard. The sad man speaks musically to his soul, because what he does say to it therein – within himself – will be heard – then and therefore – exactly as it is said. The man speaks to his soul, and listens to himself – by means of his soul – in suffering. And this in turn becomes sound and song and sadness and sweetness. We say then that the soul acts as it hears its own sound, in reflection: in reflexive action. And we notice as we have been noticing consistently and cumulatively through this study, that it is music – that it is musical analogy – that is showing this to us. And that what it shows is at the expense – at the direct expense – of words, and of meaning in language. If music had played no part; if the Psalmist had not been the Psalmist and played and sung, but the scribe; then the Psalms would not be what they are but rather a confusing and disturbing invitation to question what the Christian God allows to happen to his people, and to people in general. We mean the problem of evil, and how Christianity's detractors have always used the problem of evil to attempt to disprove the Christian God's existence or simply to cause his followers to abandon him on its basis. Yet the introduction of the Psalms at the critical juncture in the Bible, between the Old Testament and the New, stops in its tracks the ethical argument against God which constructs itself from the stories and inconsistencies of the Old Testament (and which was familiar to Augustine from his time as a Manichean Hearer; the Manichees having developed the argument to a fine pitch), and forces us to meet it with what we already know and accept and extoll in music's romanticizing of pain.

To play on the chitara is the image of the Christian faithful working corporeally, but there would be no such acts of the body if there were not first the soul to move it. We say thus that the image must be completed in its reflection. To understand then where is the location of this reflection, we need to know who it is who asks of the soul why it is sad. This cannot be the body, which simply lacks the faculty to ask. No, it is instead the mind, seat of reason and intellect and where resides the image of God. It is the mind which speaks to the soul and asks it why it is sad.

This question from the mind that is conscious of its mortality, and which is played out upon the chitara, is duplicated in the image of Christ when, before the Passion, he said to his disciples: 'My soul is overwhelmed with sorrow to the point of death.'[89] This was Christ's man-like response to the men who were interrogating him. The man who questions his mortality and plays upon the chitara imitates the questioning of the Son in the Passion and gives his response. The soul of the Saviour was sad unto death because even for Christ there could not be anything beyond death.[90]

The question, 'Why are you downcast, O my soul?', as developed in Augustine's commentaries on the Psalms, features also in his *De musica*, at the point where he is investigating in that book the sadness of the soul, its passions and its difficulties in relationship with the body, with sound and with music. These same difficulties (between the soul and the body) and the questions they generate receive their final treatment and explanation in the theory of perception that Augustine presents in *De musica*. The points of departure are the same there as in his commentaries on the Psalms. The mystery of God-made-Man and individual experience. Before the fall, and sin, the soul piloted the body without problems. But afterwards, it could only be done with great effort and tiresomely. That is, until God crushed it in his taking upon himself in bodily form the sufferings of men.[91] However, thus incarnated, even he was pressed to ask: 'Why are you downcast, O my soul?' The incarnation as recounted in Book VI of *De musica* is, in the theory of the perception of sound, bound up then with individual experience. The soul acts within the body which suffers. 'The soul dominates the fragile body by an act of conscience'[92] and when it wants to, goes outside the body by means of the body's pleasure. From this pleasure of the body, so too does the soul derive pleasure, so long as the movements of the body are not passionate. In this movement of the soul outside, towards a good that, by the contentment brought upon the body, brings contentment also upon the soul, it therefore really in fact turns inside. That is, from the pleasure gained bodily, externally, the soul comes to understand better its internal self. Naturally, the action of the soul on the body is different to the degree that it is directed towards what is sweet and what is bitter.

The soul affects the body easily when the sounds that it hears are sweet, when that which it touches appears tender, when that which it tastes is satisfying. When the actions commanded by the soul are in response easy, sweet, tender, then the soul knows that it is being in harmony with the object that those actions present to it. The soul comprehends that it is in tune and in correspondence with the object of its love. The soul 'has put its true body into contact with a suitable body outside it.'[93] In silence, it anticipates the sweet sound in hearing, and the sweet body in touch; and then it puts itself in motion towards it.[94] 'The action is accomplished in greater consciousness by virtue of the external stimulus, and given the convenience of the object, it produces a sensation of pleasure.'[95] It is as though the sweet sound and the tender touch grow our conscience: the objects sweet to our hearing, to our touch, to our taste to our vision and to our smell 'generate pleasure in him [the soul] who uses them properly';[96] and in this way do they modify the soul.

On the other hand, the soul is seen by Augustine to have difficulty influencing the body when 'the sensations which are introduced to the body or which present themselves to it cause in that body reactions that block the soul's affect.'[97] The soul warns that the object is dissonant and sour, attempting discomfort and pain.[98] If the soul must then resist that of which it is warning, we say that it and the object are not suited.

As it came towards the hour of death, the soul of Christ suffered like a body hit by a dissonant sound or by a violent punch. Augustine's theory of perception permits us to understand now the words of God in his human nature. 'The soul can no longer remain quiet during a modification of its body'[99] – and so then did Christ say that his soul was downcast in the moment of his Passion. The sweet sound moves the soul in a manner correspondingly sweet, while a sour note disturbs it painfully. The experience of sound explains by analogy the sacred mysteries and, once again, Augustine departs from a musical experience the better to give us a theological explanation.

The musical image of the 'man-chitara' will recur in the centuries following Augustine as a means of expressing the suffering human nature of the Son of God. Take for example Bonaventura (c. 1217–74), who will make Christ's last seven words upon the cross into words intoned upon the chitara, such that to each word will correspond one of the strings on the instrument.[100] The chitara will come to have for Bonaventura, then, the same symbolic significance as that conferred upon it by Augustine. It is the Son in his human nature, not in his divine nature, who asks of the Father why he abandons him.[101] It is, quite simply, the musical image of earthly life.

Take up your harp, fulfil the law

> But don't just turn your gaze to the Heavens that God has made, or to his precepts that he has given you, or to the celestial doctrine with which he has responded to you, and which he has taught to you providently, from out of the source of its truth. Take up your harp and sing to the Saviour on its ten strings. For ten are the commandments of the law: and therefore in exact relation to those ten commandments, stand the ten strings of the harp. This accord is perfection. In fact, you will find that the love of God is enjoined in three of the precepts, and the love of neighbour in seven. And surely you know, having heard it said by the Saviour, that 'All the Law and the Prophets hang on these two commandments.' (Matt. 22, 40) God is telling you from on high that 'The Lord your God is the only God': here is one string. 'Do not pronounce in vain the name of the Lord': here is the second string ... All of these are commandments of God, which have been given in his Wisdom, and which resound from on high. Take up your harp, fulfil the law, that the Lord your God came to fulfil, not to abrogate. (cf. Matt. 5, 17)[102]

As, then, with the seven words 'played/sounded' on the cross, in accordance with the seven strings of the chitara, we have here the ten strings of the harp. The instrument of David, of the King who called to himself the inspiration to compose and to sing the Psalms, allegorizes the ancient law as carried to completion in the New Law. For Augustine, the delivering of the commandments becomes a sonorous act on the part of God, playing upon the harp. Not any more is it the Son who pronounces his final words on the chitara but the Father, who delivers the words of the law to men by playing upon a stringed instrument that resonates in the heart of the Christian. When 'God speaks to you from on high' the first of his commandments, 'here is one string.'[103] Augustine believes that the delivery of the Divine commandments in this way, through musical analogy, in which the word of God plays upon a specific instrument, confers to the Word a greater degree of interiorization when it comes to the hearer.

The analogy between the ten commandments and the ten strings of the harp transforms the musical instrument into the place of Divine expression. Not only is it that God speaks from on high a command by means of the strings of the (human) heart – God's instrument – but that man, turning his gaze to the Divine precepts, himself plays upon the harp.[104] The harp symbolizes the Divine Law that, descending from above, infills the hearts of men, while becoming also their elevation as they choose then to act in accordance with it on earth. Because the ten commandments have been transmitted by the strings of the musical instrument directly to the hearts of the faithful, it is incumbent upon them – it is meet and proper – that they observe this celestial doctrine by singing to the Lord on their own harps of ten strings. The reciprocity between God and man finds expression in the musical image: God plays, and man responds by himself playing.

By this point, we can see that Augustine has developed three types of relationship between the musical instrument and the law: one holding in the Old Testament, one holding in the New Testament and one in which man imitates Christ. The commandments resound from on high, and God makes himself man and comes to earth to fulfil the law, and then, in imitation of Christ, man realizes the law himself: 'Take up your harp, fulfil the law.'[105] The analogical relationship gives birth to an operative music. The playing of the harp is not the cause of the fulfilment of the law: rather, the musical act of it plus the sonorous image resulting indicates and represents its fulfilment. In the musical image, *to celebrate* God on a musical instrument becomes the same thing as *to realize (the Law)*; because *to play* means the same in the image as *to work*; and *to take up* the instrument is the same thing as *to fulfil (the Law)*.

Thus, two key moments in the Judeo-Christian story of God – namely, the giving of the Law and the Incarnation – are condensed into musical metaphor and brought to the human level. Every time that man is within the Law, he plays the harp in a musical act that beholds the beauty of Divine justice.[106] The aesthetic dimension is no longer expressed here in the sweetness of the Divine Wisdom understood as the melodious sound of the splendid order of all things, but in the beauty of that Divine justice. Man sings upon the harp and realizes the precepts of love that comprise the ten commandments – 'The entire Law is summed up in a single command: "Love your neighbour as yourself".'[107] The sound of the harp unites itself to the words and to the voice, that together they might realize the Precept of Love that fulfils the Law of Love. Without love, man resounds like a mere cymbal, which can signify nothing: 'If I speak in the tongues of men and of angels, but have not love, I am only a resounding gong or a clanging cymbal.'[108] The song on the harp, by sharp contrast, takes upon itself in its sonorous operation to signify the love-nucleus of the commandments.

In the image of the musical metaphor (Divine and human), the man of music responds in kind to the sound of the chitara of Christ on the cross by following his example in prayer, and by echoing the sound of the harp of God by following the commandments. Augustine the theologian finds that he is being served well by the musical image, and that musical analogies confer truth by being the undeniable real-life proofs of it; and that they therefore also deliver up principles of basic faith. The most perfect form of imitation becomes that of echoing sound that repeats faithfully the source of its (own) sound. In this way, the man-chitara imitates Christ in his prayer to his Father, while the man-harp conforms voluntarily to the Father in respect of the commandments that now vibrate in his heart unto the example of Christ.

'Happy is the harp, but take up the chitara'

> 'Happy is the harp', but take up the chitara. The Psalmist says in so many words what he has said before: 'Take the psalm and give the timbral.' Here, in the place of the Psalm, we find the harp, and in the place of the timbral, the chitara. Of this, however, we are admonished, that to the preaching of God's word we make answer by bodily works.[109]

Augustine repeats here the allegorical distinction developed in his commentary on Psalm 32, between the harp and the chitara.

The harp belongs to the heavens, the chitara to the earth. The first indicates the Word of God and the preaching of it, the second, earthly works. However, because the Christian lives in anticipation of the Kingdom-to-Come, he must proceed for now on earth by works: 'Happy is the harp, but take up the chitara.'[110] To receive, or to 'take up', is inseparable from giving, as the harp is inseparable from the chitara. The celestial musical instrument is happy only insofar as it vibrates in sympathy with the earth. If there were not this earthly and material resonance, there would be neither anticipation nor joy in things celestial and spiritual.

The third verse of the Psalm duplicates the invitation to respond with works to the preaching of the Divine Word: to the Psalm corresponds the harp, to the timbral the chitara. 'The timbral, insofar as it is made from leather, is an object that registers in the sphere of the carnal.'[111] The Psalm is spiritual, the timbral carnal; the song is spiritual, the instrument is corporeal; and in verse five of Psalm 80, we are exactly invited to take up the things spiritual and offer the things corporeal: 'Receive the voice and give the works'.[112] In the same way that the spiritual voice is inseparable from the material sound of the instrument, the celestial harp is inseparable from the earthly chitara.

The musical image of the harp in relationship to the Law is enriched with another signification which this time we find in Augustine's commentary on Psalm 91. This commentary begins with the distinction between the harp and song, from there to make the musical image the place in which shall be differentiated the Christian faith from the Hebrew. To the standing distinction between the chitara and the harp, is added that of the harp and the song; as between action, represented in the harp, and the word of confession, as represented in the song. In this way, we are made to see also something of the historical valorization of accompanying song; in that it is made to express the proper thought concurrent with action, and therefore the musical image in toto of the man, in whom there is perfect coherence between his words and his actions.

In confessing himself to God, the Christian sings; in just works, he plays the musical instrument: 'to play is to work,' while to confess is to sing to God both in prosperity and tribulation.[113]

It is good to praise the Lord and make music to your name, O Most High, to proclaim your love in the morning and your faithfulness at night, to the music of the ten-stringed harp and the song of the chitara.[114]

To sing the name of the Lord is to confess that sins proceed from man and that good works proceed from God.[115] And that every good action guided by love declares the name of man in Heaven: 'Therefore praise with the harp the name of the Lord, if you want your name to be with security with God in Heaven.'[116]

As we are noting, the musical image acquires a supplementary dimension in the contrast between the Christian and Hebrew faiths. And it is this that Augustine introduces in his commentary on Psalm 91 with the concept of 'carrying the harp'.

The ten-stringed harp represents the ten commandments of the Law. But these must be sung out on the harp; it is not enough that the harp is simply carried about. For the Jews, too, have the Law: but they carry it about thus and do not sing it out.[117]

The musical image of the harp contains within it the true characteristics of the Christian faith insofar as they can be seen in musical symbolism. Thus, the contrast with the old, Hebrew Law; with the new Law of Love; with works; and with joyous affection.

The difference between the musical act of singing on the instrument and the, as it were, 'pre-musical' act of simply carrying it about signifies the practice of the Law – the light yoke – on the part of the Christians, while the Hebrews, not yet able to make music, find themselves under the heavy yoke of the Law. They carry about with them the Instrument-Law without playing it or singing it. *To sing* becomes synonymous with the *practice* of the Law, which means that *to sing* means also *to possess love*. 'Therefore those who do not have love can, yes, carry the harp, but they cannot sing.'[118] Thus comes to be stated again in enhanced form, the connection between song and love.

In this Christian allegory of the Law, the song on the harp is not merely the practice of it but also the happiness of it, because love is indissociable from joy. Augustine will in fact incorporate a passage from Saint Paul in order the better to commentate on the joy of practising the Law and the way that joy features, therefore, in its musical allegory:

> 'For God loves a cheerful giver'. (2 Cor 9, 7) Whatever it is that you do, do it with happiness. In other words, do the good, and do it well. If, instead, you work grudgingly, in sadness, and notwithstanding that your resulting works do good of themselves, it is not you who now do them: he who does not sing, destroys the harp.[119]

The song contains the affection of joyous love, and yet again we see how the particularity of the Christian message finds its analogue in the singularity of music, with regard to the former's indissoluble union of word and affection in the spoken word. If you practise the Law without joy, you do not sing. If you work the good with a bad heart, you do not work the good on the harp. He who plays practices the good joyously – that is, practices the good, well – because playing is the sign of gaiety (*In psallendo enim hilaritus est*[120]). The affection of the song determines the value of the action that must accompany the just words of man, and this dimension also finds, in Augustine, its musical allegory. For it is with reference to this that Augustine interprets the words from the Psalm (91) that go: 'With a song, on the chitara'.

In the context of Psalm 91, 'with a song' signifies 'with the words', while 'on the chitara' signifies 'with works'. Whoever speaks without works possesses only the song, while whoever works without speaking possesses only the chitara.

> If you speak only words, it is as though you had only the song, without the chitara. If you work but do not also speak, it is as though you had only the chitara. For this reason we are enjoined to speak well and work well, if we want to have the song together with the chitara.[121]

It is the responsibility of man to use well his words and to harmonize them with his actions, and to do this in the image of the player who sings upon his musical instrument and in whom, therefore, there can be no disunity between word and action.

As we cannot (now) conceptualize the song without the chitara, so too can we not think of the harp without the chitara. The chitara and the harp have in fact an allegorical sense which testifies to the two indissociable elements in the Christian message. The Psalmist does not present to the reader a simple pairing of musical instruments – *canticum cum chitara* plus *psalterium iucundum cum chitara* – but uses the image of their musical coupling to indicate a message that requires to be deciphered at the level of symbolism. In Augustine's interpretation, the musical image *canticum cum chitara* places in metaphor a moral precept and contains the ideal of the Christian life in the union of words and actions. In this Christian precept, allegorized in music, we see mirrored the practice of music that unites word with instrumental sound and which comprises then a variety of theological concepts. The praise befitting the name of God, the fulfilment of the Law, the joyous affection that is indispensable both to working and speaking well: all of these flow together in music to become the image of the Law and of its *Mass*, in love and in happiness.

The coupling of musical terms in the Psalms accounts for a plurality of significations up to and including speaking of man in his entirety. Psalm and timbral, song and chitara, harp and chitara reach out to the pairings of spirit and body, soul and body, thoughts and acts, words and acts, Heaven and earth, God and man, Father and Son, glory and humility, joy and sadness.

The musical image speaks of man, of the Son and of the Father. While the works of man on the chitara make echo of the prayers of the Son to the Father, at that time when his Passion intoned painfully upon the strings of the cross. The works on the harp, on the other hand, follow the Divine Law as Christ followed the Will of his Father. And so does the man as chitara and harp resound in imitation of the suffering Christ in the glory of his tribulation. To the ineffable song of God responds human praise in all ages – 'Take up the harp by obeying the commandments; take up the chitara by enduring the passions.'[122] Not only do the sung praises to God depart from silence and affection, and return there afterwards, but simultaneously does the silent song of the loving and conscious soul respond to the ineffable song of the Father. The voice of consciousness IS the 'internal Voice of God (God's Voice in us: God's instructing Voice in us)'.[123]

If the song of praise underlines the importance of listening, of love and of consciousness, the image of the musical instruments makes for an allegorical mirror on action. The circular relationship between God and man is condensed in musical metaphor. The chitara and the harp become symbols while the musical images of God express a reality that bursts the senses, the reasoning and the intellect of man by means of a sonorous hypostasis. We will see in the final chapter how Augustine deepens this theme when he conceptualizes the God who sings and plays the (human body).

We are definitely not talking of a Creator God thought of in the image of a musical demiurge! God sends the Law, he incarnates it, he suffers on the cross, he renders his Spirit – 'And when Jesus had cried out again in a loud voice, he gave up his Spirit' (Matt. 27, 50) – in sonorous acts, and Being responds to God in music. The musical man is no longer – a là Classical type – he who brings into accord the diverse faculties of his soul and who tempers his passions, but he who plays in all circumstances in response to the constant operations of the Divine and who does not then 'break the chitara'. Made in the image of a musical God, and always active in his performative listening and in his transformative music, the musical man ceases neither to sing (to confess, to praise, to love) nor to play (to work, to fulfil, to love).

Ultimately, to the musical image that contains the contrasting affections (joy and sadness, happiness and tribulation), love, listening, consciousness, confession, works, the fulfilment of the Law and therefore the union of the earth with the Heavens and of man with God, Augustine gives also a special place to *sound*. The sound of the musical instruments as a metaphor for human action does not just convey affection, but elevates it to God and allows him to take joy in the musical sound of man. On the Psalmodic theme of Divine listening, to the God who turns his ear to the prayers of man, Augustine adds the God who takes joint pleasure in the musical sound of man, whether made upon the chitara or the harp. We will see in the final chapter that you cannot appreciate the full importance of sound for Augustine in these contexts without analysing the ineffable musical sound of God Himself, which Augustine describes in various commentaries on the Psalms. However, before we turn to the man of music, perfected in silent Being, and before we consider the Augustinian musical concept of the Father, we must examine three other musical men: the Prophet, the Saint and Christ in his human nature.

2

The Prophet and the Saint

In the biblical text, music has a privileged place when it comes to prophecy and, in Hebrew thought, the prophet comes to be thought of as a musical instrument predestined by God. This musical metaphor helps to bring to the foreground notions like inspiration and the prophetic word. The prophetic word is supernatural. It announces future events and generally speaks things which man could have no way of knowing otherwise. Music often serves to register the exceptionality of this word, inspired from the Heavens. David is the greatest example of this: 'The prophet sings of future events, expressing them in the way of an augur.'[1] Moreover, in order to compose the Psalms, David invokes the Divine inspiration by means of his corded instrument; and so we see in the iconography that he is represented with an upturned countenance while playing on his harp (or psalter). The King receives the Holy Spirit and glimpses the angelic choir. The music performed by this choir allows him to hear by it, yet another music. And so he becomes the receptacle of this other, angelic but (otherwise) inaudible music. Again, his playing on his harp opens the door to this 'listening-in-on-the-angelic-inaudible', which in turn he is able to 'make back' into the words of the Psalms we know; their inspired words having been received in his interior listening.

At work in the prophetic word is the spiritual listening, made possible by the music which disposes the being (the prophet) to receive the prophetic spirit – a 'listening in spirit'.[2] With this expression, Augustine distinguishes sonorous listening from secret listening. That is, the prophetic listening takes place within the sanctuary of mystery where resounds the Silent Word. These words are not heard by men: men only get to listen to them in prophecy and lend them their faith without having heard them directly.[3] In secret, the prophet hears that which he will then prophecy openly, in the same way that the Christian man – the Christian man of music – listens in spirit to the things said in his intimate interior in silent voice.

The Davidic music participates also in another experience, not of the inspirited words but of the disturbance of inspiration per se and the disturbance of the word. This would be the distorted and out-of-tune word of Saul. Saul, invaded by demonic spirits, loses the Divine spirit. In prey to melancholy, his interior vision is obscured. In order to reinstate coherence and peace in his soul, he calls on the intervention of music. David plays for Saul and cures him thanks to his music.

> Whenever the spirit from God came upon Saul, David would take his harp and play. Then relief would come to Saul; he would feel better, and the evil spirit would leave him.[4]

In the dyscrasia of the musical man, music can serve to reharmonize against the malady, and the biblical passage just cited did in fact serve to justify just this use of music in medicine and treatment for centuries.

Indeed another prophet, Elisha, will demand the help of a musician: '"But now bring me a harpist." While the harpist was playing, the hand of the Lord came upon Elisha.'[5] Without music, Elisha could not receive the Spirit. The music attracted the Divine Word and disposed the mind of the prophet to receive it. The authority of David who composed the Psalms to the sound of his musical instrument and of Elisha, who prophesized to the sound of music, both serve to establish the relationship between music and the inspired word; between the peculiar power of musical sound (in general) and the particularity of the Divine Word as transmitted to the prophet.

The words of the sung Psalm are Divine by inspiration and human by enunciation. They are not of man insofar as they are of the Spirit, and they are of man insofar as they 'groan' as one who suffers. In the Psalms of passion, the sung words are words of tears and pain, yet they are the words of Him (God) who does not cry or suffer. The merciful speaks by means of the miserable, and in the song the voice is therefore human and also not human because it proceeds from the Spirit.[6] It is therefore in the perspective of the Divine Voice – human and non-human – plus the power of song, that the Psalms are sung. And by drawing on this biblical backdrop united to music as the means of attracting and receiving the Spirit, the authors of the Judeo-Christian tradition paint the image of the prophet, transformed into a musical instrument.

The body of the prophet as played by the invisible musician

The prophet is, essentially, a voice. A voice that cries in the desert. A voice crying an oftentimes incomprehensible Word – incomprehensible because it is so dense, so rich, so hermetic. The prophet encloses within himself the voice of God transmitted through his, the prophet's voice, as the chosen instrument of God. Through the prophet's voice, is heard that which the Spirit has placed within the prophet.[7] And this supernatural Word spoken by the prophet brings with it various musical questions. For the prophets have been elevated by God to the musical dimension. Their minds have been made to resound musically while their bodies have been transformed into musical instruments. Before Augustine, Philo of Alexandria, among others, offered a testimony of these two instruments – mind and body – in his *Quis rerum divinarum heres sit*.[8] The theme of the man-turned-musical instrument would become a classic of philosophical and theological literature. For example, Guglielmo di Saint-Thierry (1085–1148) would re-propose the whole idea of the musical metaphor, as developed along these lines of the body of man transformed into a musical instrument, plucked by the plectrum of the soul.[9]

Quis rerum divinarum heres sit begins with some considerations on language and its limits.

> The most violent passions, as in joy extraordinary, we leave without words ... For this, Moses confessed to have remained with 'weak voice' and with 'heavy language' (Ex 4, 10) from the moment that God took him to speak with him.[10]

Such silence can be a sign of stupefaction. From the Divine voice, to the prophetic word, to the pain inexpressible or to the joy unbearable, the being (the human being) is not able to turn the experience into words. Philo follows this with a physico-psychological description of this state in which the wonder of it provokes a kind of weakness. This stupor leaves its patient without voice. What would be needed instead would be a kind of language that would better correspond with this emotive state of violent passions and extraordinary joys. A non-discursive language that would take over and fill up the silence of voice otherwise. (The silence which we find so strongly depicted and promoted in Augustine's writings; his priority generally being the pastoral one of dissuading his readers and parishioners from dabbling in these matters, or worse, from seeking out some soothsayer to dabble for them.) For Philo, this would be a 'free[wheeling] course of thought', because this freewheeling course would come closest to pure emotion.

Because worded language is simply not consonant enough with human affection, what is required is an articulation more 'agile' and 'sublime'. This would be able to represent 'the beauty of thoughts rather than of words'.[11] In this context, Philo commentates the command of Moses to 'Be silent, O Israel, and listen!'[12] More than the literal sense, Philo develops the allegorical sense of silence and of listening in the soul. He begins from an everyday experience, so to speak, in order to arrive at a spiritual precept. Take, for example, the distracted listening of one who listens to another talking, but who's mind is elsewhere.[13] The private or political matters that the listener is enumerating mentally while the other is talking generate confusion in the listener's mind: the one who is talking is heard, but not listened to, and the situation becomes a paragon for Philo therefore, of the pupa without a soul who has ears, but does not hear.[14]

Only he who mentally and spiritually draws close upon he who talks, and makes himself silent, according to the precept of Moses, will be able to truly hear.[15] This active listening – Augustine's, 'wise listening'; as we know from earlier in this book – is necessary in order to hear the other and the Divine. And only he who knows how to listen in silence may speak. In this silence resounds the cry of the soul: deprived of sound, but musical nonetheless. Philo distinguishes then two human voices: the exterior and the interior, the sonorous and the silent, the body and the soul. In the resounding silence of the soul, the instrument of communication 'is perfectly adapted in harmony to its needs and fitted with a powerful voice'.[16] For Augustine, this voice is audible to God but also to those who have drawn close in heart to the 'speaker'. For both Augustine and Philo, admirers of Plato, intelligible (silent) music is superior to sensible music and it frees the thoughts from the words and it expresses them through a music itself also now liberated from the limitations of sound. Silent, capable of being heard only by the consciousness stretched out towards it – towards its intention and its heart. 'Only he who knows how to listen to the intelligible music is capable of taking hold of the harmonious concert and the song of the soul.'[17] The silent voice of he who does know how falls silent the better to hear *The Other*, and the Divine resounds in musical mode. To characterize the voice of the soul, Philo uses the concepts of harmony, concert, song and music. And he defines the technical characteristics of the latter.

> When the instrument of the mind, in its entirety, makes to sound within itself a chord of one or two octaves, He Who listens asks: 'Why do you cry out to me?'[18]

The cry of the soul that is heard by God and God's response in his question – Why do you cry out to me? – are both equally over and above spoken language. They are musical and silent. This brief passage from Philo shows us the perfect circularity of speculative listening as it takes place between God and man – always in musical metaphor. Man cries to God on high because God's ears are turned towards him;[19] while vice versa, God's ears are only so turned because man continues to call out to him.[20] The musical mind – the mind of the musical man – as it invokes the Divine listening – the Divine response – as well as the original musical cry of the soul to God: all of this is expressed in the perfect interval, the *Octave*, that reunites in itself all of the intervals and which contains in itself in potential, all of the musical sounds. From silence comes a silent musical cry, audible by him only who knows how to hear it by the voice of his soul.

To the soul that intones a perfect *interval-cry*, the body acts as a sonorous pendant. And so we see that we have now reached the stage at which the musical metaphor is placed within the theme of *Ecstasy*. Of the four forms of ecstasy – the delirious furore, the deep daze, the wise calm and the divine possession[21] – Philo places music in relationship to the last. Once again, we are in a context most strictly tied to the word. But not anymore with regard to the impossibility of speaking, or to intelligible music and the silence of the soul, but to the word that speaks the unknowable. That is, the future that cannot yet be known to man. The voice of the prophet is really the voice of another passing through by means of it: *The Other Who* inspires what is said. Whoever prophecies, is an instrument in the hands of God. This interpreter of God 'is the sonorous instrument of God, played and solicited by him in ways invisible'.[22]

The prophetic Word inspired by God in men good and wise that he selects to be its interpreters is therefore the word emitted by a musical body. The musical instrument is confounded with the voice of the prophet (issuing from it) and the musical sound with the sounds articulated in speech by the prophetic voice. In this way, God is served,

> by the organs of the voice, of the mouth and of the tongue and with arts invisible and harmonious, which he overmasters in order to make of them musical instruments most melodious, and rich in every harmony.[23]

God is the invisible musician who plays in order to be heard. The word of the prophet exits from his vocal organs insofar as they have now been transformed into musical instruments capable of every harmony when once they are struck and played by God. Thus music comes to affirm in its supernaturality of language, what is exceptional in the gift of prophecy.

The human word of the soul-turned-to-God and inaudible to men is mirrored in this supernatural Word inspired by God and very much turned to men. For Philo, both belong within the musical dimension. The first voice is full of the perfect intervals that enclose all of the (possible) musical sounds within a silent cry that reaches out to the Divine ears that incline themselves to all such questions (cries). The second voice is expressed in a sonorous, audible, bodily voice that is capable of all the harmonies because it is being played (directly and invisibly) by God. The intelligible music of the brimming soul that is turned towards God finds its sonorous echo in the bodies of the prophets, rich in every harmony.

The singularity of the message – the faithful invocation by the prophet-man or the announcement of the future – is indicated precisely in its musical enunciation. Thus, the musical image takes in themes and questions of affective language as well as the limits of rational, discursive language. Later, we will come to see how these Judeo-Christian reflections on language will be completed in the theme of the ineffable, both at the aesthetic and theological level.

The re-interpretation of the Platonic musical soul, the bond between the exceptionality of prophetic language and music, the image of the body as musical instrument were all of them theological and musical themes dear to Augustine. The musical word figures at the heart of his portrayal of man as possessing a soul that can know how to make itself heard on high, and a body open to the Divine word by means of it having given its sound box to it in abandonment. In the Judeo-Christian tradition, under the influence of Plato, the musical image invigorates the various levels of dialogue between God and man. And also, then, the Saint, another figure in privileged relationship to God, and likewise best thought of, then, in musical analogy.

The harmony of the saints: Voice, wind and percussion

The saints who rest in God sing and play all types of musical instrument. Not only do they form up in a choir and use the stringed instruments, the wind instruments and percussion, but they are themselves transformed into musical instruments. Augustine's commentaries on Psalms 32, 42, 80 and 91, which describe the musical man, receive their full elaboration in his commentary on Psalm 150, especially the last passage of that Psalm, in its intrinsic musicality:

> Praise him with the sounding of the trumpet, praise him with the harp and the chitara, praise him with tambourine and dancing, praise him with the strings and flute, praise him with the clash of cymbals, praise him with resounding cymbals. Let everything that have breath praise the Lord.[24]

This last Psalm is a veritable musical hyperbole of praise! Augustine will interpret allegorically one after the other of the instruments – all of them made into allegories of the saints. In this way, the contemporary reader, by immersing themselves in Augustine's biblical commentaries, gets to see musical images dressed in their full theological significations.

Initially, at the first semantic level, Augustine will limit himself to superficial analogy: one praises on the sound of the trumpets because if their 'unbeatable impact'.[25] Here, the chief characteristics and requirements of praise meet straightforwardly with the same in the instrument. The trumpet is by nature, look and sound the obvious and classic symbol and analogy of human praise. Augustine accepts this for what it is and doesn't add anything to it. Next, Augustine deduces from the Psalm a new interpretation of the harp that in fact completes that begun in his commentary on Psalm 32. This shows us the polysemic symbolism of musical images. In this new interpretation, Augustine reasons that with the harp being already established as the instrument that praise God from on high, and the chitara as the instrument that does so from below, the harp might be thought of also as a metaphor for the celestial creation, and the chitara, obviously, then, for those of the earth. To the chitara and the harp he then adds the timbral, which in his commentary on Psalm 80 he makes stand for the corporeal universe and in his commentary on Psalm 33, for the Passion of Christ. While in Psalm 150, it represents the transformation of the flesh.[26]

The corporeal universe, the Passion and the transformation of the flesh, none of these contradict each other for being signified by the timbral, but rather they enrich each other each time; with each symbolism drawing from a property that all really do share in common, and which they share in turn, then, with the known properties of the timbral as an instrument of musical sound. For example, if the timbral is made from stretched skin, then it has been made in the image of Christ on the cross, while, when used in praising the saints, the timbral represents the flesh transformed and liberated from earthly corruption – 'When in-corruption will have devoured the corruption'.[27] In the final transformation, the body will not suffer any more and the flesh will be liberated from the miseries of earthly corruption necessitated by original sin. Thus will the saints live, transfigured in Eternity.[28]

As the animal skin is transformed into a new reality in the making of the timbral, so too is Christ on the cross 'stretched' to resound in a new way and to bring life through death. The transformation of the animal skin in making the musical instrument offers an image comprehensible and tactile to the senses. The musical image allows to be put onto the human level a mystery of the faith – such as life through death – or a truth of the faith – such as the resurrection of the body and the life eternal – and permits man to draw near to them.

The praise sung upon musical instruments liberated from corruption, in other words, the praise made upon transformed bodies, transforms, reforms in the image of the Creator and then conforms man to the glory of the resurrection.[29] The idea of the flesh that is free from corruption is very much found in Augustine's commentaries in connection with the idea of praise sung upon the stringed instruments. For the strings of these instruments are after all made from animals, but of course transformed for their new purpose: 'The strings are of flesh, but by now extinct of corruption'.[30] While the praise made upon these incorruptible instruments is joined by necessity with the body (the human body of the musician, and the body of the instrument, and the musician's body as instrument) (*in chordis et organo*). In commentating the couplet *in chordis et organo*, Augustine will pull focus upon how the word *organo* should be interpreted. In this case, not any longer as the single instrument (*organa*) but as the generic word for designating all the instruments (*organum*). This leads into his conclusion that musical instruments should not be played in isolation but together in their diversity, thus giving a picture of the saints in Heaven, each one of them unique, but together in harmony.[31]

This musical image is carried on further and justified by the theological analogy of the concert of the saints in Heaven as like so many stars that shine resplendently differently.[32] As always, Augustine shows himself happy and proud to follow the Apostle when it comes to analogical interpretation. Here, the image of the stars shining resplendently differently accelerates his musical analogy. The saints with God in Heaven shine by playing together musically in concord, as is anticipated in the concert of musical instruments described in Psalm 150:

> 'Praise Him on the strings and organ.' (*in chordis et organo*) Both harp and chitara, which have been mentioned above, have strings. But 'organ' is a general name for all instruments of music, although usage has now obtained that those are specially

called organ which are inflated with bellows: but I do not think that this kind is meant here. For since organ is a Greek word, applied generally, as I have said, to all musical instruments, this instrument, to which bellows are applied, is called by the Greeks by another name: but it being called organ is rather a Latin and conversational usage. When then he says, 'on the strings and organ,' he seems to me to have intended to signify some instrument which has strings. For it is not harps and chitaras only that have strings: but, because in the chitara, and harp, on account of the sound from things below and things above, somewhat has been found which can be understood after this distinction, he has suggested to us to seek some other meaning in the strings themselves: for they too are flesh, but flesh now set free from corruption. And to those, it may be, he added the organ, to signify that they sound not each separately, but sound together in most harmonious diversity, just as they are arranged in a musical instrument. For even then the saints of God will have their differences, accordant, not discordant, that is, agreeing, not disagreeing, just as sweetest harmony arises from sounds differing indeed, but not opposed to one another. 'The sun has one kind of splendour, the moon another and the stars another; and star differs from star in splendour.' (1 Cor 15, 41)[33]

The last part of the Psalm which evokes the well-tuned cymbals and the joyful cymbals – *Laudate eum in cymbalis bene sonantibus, laudate eum in cymbalis iubilationis*[34] – completes the 'community' of the metaphor by adding to it the person of the saint, in his type as a man of music. Augustine gives two metaphorical interpretations of the well-tuned cymbals, but preferring the second of them. The first is that the cymbals, in being struck one against the other to make the sound, represent the lips. The second is that the cymbals (in their comparative autonomy vis-à-vis the stringed instruments) represent the honour, received without asking. The cymbals of joy, on the other hand, invoke interiority. They are played in the soul. Augustine defines joy in this commentary as he does in his commentary on Psalm 32.[35] Joy is 'ineffable praise'.[36] Therefore, the expression 'cymbals of joy' refers to the unspeakable. The ineffable can only express itself in the soul.[37] And the praise of the ineffable draws on the soul, translating into silence that which is concealed therein, offering it on the altar of interiority.

Augustine melts the literal sense of the Psalmodic words and images in order to draw from them the allegorical sense and to put before the reader the hidden significations. As the harp acquires its whole other, higher dimension in its symbolism, so too now the cymbal as well as the act of playing it. To play 'on the cymbal of joy' is to play with a love that makes it that the sound of the cymbal is no longer empty but has sense and meaning.[38] It is to play the instrument with the intelligence that distinguishes man from the animals: to play over and above the material act of playing, in alliance instead now with what is sensible to man in sound and with the soul.

> 'Praise Him on the well-sounding cymbals, praise Him on cymbals of jubilation'. Cymbals touch one another in order to sound, and therefore are by some compared to our lips. But I think it better to understand that God is in a manner praised on the cymbal, when each is honoured by his neighbour, not by himself, and then honouring one another, they give praise to God. But lest any should understand such cymbals as sound without life, therefore I think he added, 'on cymbals of jubilation.' For 'jubilation' that is, unspeakable praise, proceeds not, save from life.[39]

Finally, Augustine considers the musical metaphors of the mind, of the spirit and of the body. With these, he makes his beginning with musical theory, rather than with the saints. Augustine starts from the tripartite division of (1) musical sound in voice, (2) wind instruments and (3) percussion (*voce, flatu, pulsu*). The Psalm in its complexity mentions all three types of sound, and, by analogy, refers them to the mind, the spirit and the body.[40] The voice articulated in song stands to the mind that expresses concepts as the wind instruments (*flatu*) stand to the human spirit, while the instruments of percussion (*pulsu*) represent the body, with its heartbeats that give life.

Man is turned into a 'concert'. His voice allegorizes the thoughts of his mind; his breath in the wind instruments, the blowing of his spirit; and his striking of the instruments of percussion, the beats of his body. The Divine wind breathes into life,[41] gives the Spirit, articulates the voice and puts rhythm into the body. And Augustine's commentary will conclude by turning to the first words of the Psalm, *Laudate Dominum in sanctis eius*.[42] The invitation to praise God in his saints is returned to those same saints: 'You are the trumpet, the harp, the chitara, the timbral, the choir, the strings and the organ; the well-tuned cymbals and the cymbals of jubilation.'[43] Augustine reproduces the hyperbole of the final Psalm in this final 'list' in his commentary. The saints are all the instruments, just as man *is* the song of perfect praise.[44] The man of music comprises every which type of sound and in the saint resounds therefore, every which type of music.

> Nor do I think that I should pass over what musicians say, that there are three kinds of sounds, by voice, by breath, by striking: by voice, uttered by throat and windpipe, when man sings without any instrument; by breath, as by pipe, or anything of that sort: by striking, as by harp, or anything of that kind. None then of these kinds is omitted here: for there is voice in the choir, breath in the trumpet, striking in the harp, representing mind, spirit, body, but by similitudes, not in the proper sense of the words. When then he proposed, 'Praise God in His saints,' to whom said he this, save to themselves? And in whom are they to praise God, save in themselves? For you, says he, are 'His saints;' you are 'His strength,' but that which He wrought in you; you are 'His mighty works, and the multitude of His greatness,' which He has wrought and set forth in you. You are 'trumpet, psaltery, harp, timbral, choir, strings, and organ, cymbals of jubilation sounding well,' because sounding in harmony. All these are you: let nought that is vile, nought that is transitory, nought that is ludicrous, be here thought of. And since to savour of the flesh is death, 'let every spirit praise the Lord'.[45]

The musical paradigm allows Augustine to speak of man under his various aspects: soul and body, heart and spirit, intellect and reason, sentiment and affection. The musical image is charged with the cognitive and unifying power of the symbol: in the image converge realities that all compete when we speak of the Christian.

Now, in order to consider the new musical man (of the New Law) in all his complexity, we must turn to the musical images of Christ and to the concept of the 'song of the heart'. We are about to see that the metaphor we have been working of the musical *man-instrument* – man, prophet, saint – cannot in fact be separated from another image: that of Christ in his human nature, transformed into a musical instrument at the crucial moment of his Passion.

3

Christ

Man as made in the sonorous image of God cannot be separated from the Word made sound. Even if the Augustinian considerations on the Word-sound are not referred to music, they nonetheless discuss one of the questions central to musical debate in the entire course of its history. Namely, that of the relationship between word and sound, text and melody, and of both with affection. From the theological perspective, the sound is considered together with the voice and the Word – the Divine Word, the *Logos*. The reflections on word and on sound constitute the premiss of Augustinian metaphor around Christ-as-musical instrument, and around the relationship between the Passion and the world of sound.

Both the differences and the points in common between the Divine Word and the human word are one of Augustine's favourite themes. In the act of creation, in the sending of the Law and in the Incarnation, sight and hearing, as well as sound and time, are always in play. The Creating Word, coeternal with the Father, in which all the sounds are pronounced together and eternally,[1] is distinguished from the sonorous Voice, passing and material, that God makes to resound to designate his Son during the Baptism and the Transfiguration,[2] and then distinguished again from the Word in time (the Word in Scripture).[3] By using syllables disposed in time, God spoke in human language, even He Who possesses a speech that is spiritual and eternal.[4] In the Incarnation, on the other hand, God Himself descended to earth and made directly thereby sound, in order to be heard; and a body, in order to be seen and touched.

The Incarnation and the plan of salvation in music

The corporeal manifestation of God in the Incarnation represents the temporal and sensible descent of the eternally invisible:

> That which was from the beginning, which we have heard, which we have seen with our eyes, which we have looked at and our hands have touched – this we proclaim concerning the Word of life.[5]

'Assumed the sound of voice'

'The Divine Word, for the necessity of announcing itself, assumed the sound of voice to meet with the ears of its listeners.'[6] Augustine's commentary on Psalm 8, as with other of his commentaries, discusses the significance of sound as part of a semiology of the Word Incarnate. God is brought down to among men. He is made humble, like an ephemeral sound. Scripture itself is also the example of this, in that by it, God has deigned to communicate in a way as to touch human ears.

Following the usual analogical argument, Augustine places the Word Incarnate in parallel with the human word. In the same way as that when God made himself man, he did not reveal his invisible nature, but kept it secret, so too the thoughts as formulated in the secret place of a man's mind are not (actually) the thoughts themselves.[7] Nonetheless, God is seen, even if his corporeal form cannot speak for all of his true being. And by the same token, then, thoughts given out to another are transmitted (as far as they go), even if their full existence and meaning can never leave the mind of their author. This fullness always remains hidden, for it is in the very nature of words that they can succeed in translating only themselves (and therefore their agreed-upon meanings between people). Of course, it is true that around words, inflection of voice can go a long way in filling them out and extending them ('in the very sound of the voice is enclosed the significance'[8]), but it remains that neither the word nor the inflection of voice can circumscribe true thought. In the same way can nothing be said of the essence of the Divine nature.

Just as there is always something in affection and thought that is greater than human words can compass, so too in music there is always something that cannot be translated into words, something that always escapes the discourse, something of the occult that cannot be transmitted by means of the word, but rather only heard, as it is, clothed in sound. As thought transcends its sonorous perimeter, so the Divine nature is over and above whatever it is that can be said of it (in any particular moment): 'If you have understood him, he is not God.'[9] Sound speaks the humility of the human nature of God and words testify to it, but his glory 'transcends and is superior to the expressions of any word, and of every language.'[10]

The Son is the ephemeral sound of humility, the Father the eternal word of glory, but the glory is manifested in humility as the word is in sound; that same sound that reveals the secret thoughts of another and comes to be held in the memory. When the sound of the word has penetrated the ear, it thus separates inside man: 'it completes a separation, in which the sound remains with the ears, while the sense is held in the memory of those who have listened.'[11] The significance of what has been said passes through the hearing and the ears and is held in another place. This – the memory – conserves the significance which has just been pronounced by a sound now flown.

More than the distinction between the sounded word and the silent thought, in which is reflected the double nature of Christ, Augustine develops the difference between the voice and the word – principally in his interpretation of the role of John. He talks of John, the voice who cried in the desert,[12] as the 'voice of one who broke the silence'.[13] As the announcer of Christ. John is voice; Christ is Word. The first is in time, the second is in eternity. John, like any man who is a man, introduces the word into the heart by means of the sound of his voice that is inseparable from its interior movement: 'speak with the lips, but draw close with the heart.'[14] The sound of the voice penetrates the ear, its significance the mind, and the heart is touched. This was in fact a principle of classical rhetoric which would go on to be referenced in the Christian philosophical-musical literature throughout the Middle Ages. In the following passage, Augustine focuses on the complementary roles of sound and signification, of voice and word, and produces a veritable theology of sound:

If I think of that which I plan to say, the word is already inside me; but, wanting to speak to you, I seek for the way in which it might be put into your heart what is already now in mine. I seek for how it might arrive with you and find a place in your heart; as this word is now already in my heart. And so, I fall upon my voice, and speak to you. The sound of my voice bears to you the intelligence of the word; and in just this same way as the sound of my voice has borne to you the intelligence in the word, now does the sound of it pass away. But the word, borne to you by sound [which has now flown], is by now in your heart together with my heart. Consider therefore whether the sound is not in all of this really saying to you [of the word]: 'He must become greater; I must become less' (John 3, 30). The voice has given service in its vibration and then moved on, as if to say: 'That joy is mine, and it is now complete' (John 3, 29). We conserve the word. We take care of it and we do not lose the word born in the depths of Being.[15]

When the lips have vibrated and carried to the ears the breath of sound, they pull themselves back, for their whole joy was to have transmitted those vibrations of sound, knowing full well that their true significance would be conserved afterwards, in both speaker and hearer. We treasure the word of the other, the precious gift revealed in intimacy. Their thought, transmitted from their heart to ours by means of their voice. We see above how Augustine constructs an analogy – as he is wont – between the individual experience and the biblical story. The sound becomes the allegory of John who must fade away, while and in order that Christ should grow – Just as does grow and mature the word of the speaker in the heart of the receiver. In this scheme, the Son is not any more the fleeing sound of the eternal Word of the Father, but Son and Father are one Word together counterposed; Who John expresses in the transitory sound of his prophetic voice.

The sound manifests, the sound transmits an image to the mind and to the heart, and this sonorous image imprints itself in a manner superseding sound. In a manner superseding its passing in time and the syllables which mark that time and which form it as a word. The significance always transcends the letter and the emotion conveyed by the sound soars above that same sound. There is something that persists beyond the sounding of the word, and in order to hone in on this, Augustine refuses to separate the theological from the psychological, the significance of the Divine Word from the affection born in the sound of the body, the heart and the mind of man.

In his commentary on John the Evangelist, Augustine deepens this 'something' that persists in our intimacy beyond the sounding of the word – that continues to ring in our heart. The faith whose daily bread is to listen to the Word must have a clear picture in its mind of the distinction between sound and word. The Word is never extinguished, and the Word sounds eternally, and its eternal sounding is the means and the making of everything (in the Universe). Men, by contrast, have a transitory word. They have words which sound and then pass. This gives us the picture of the Eternal Word which remains in a man, even as the word of it is (being) lost (in the process of time). A picture of a Word, proffered in Spirit, that lives in a man's interior place: 'That which you perceive by sound, but which you do not identify with [mere] sound.'[16] This 'something' is clearly close to the affective dimension familiar in music – the dimension that is beyond translation into words, that is beyond even the words as they may be sung to music in song. All that can be said of it is that it imprints itself on the soul and transforms it.

Yes, *significance* cannot be derived from the mere sound of the word. It seems, in fact, that there might be a paradoxical disproportion in play. Take, for example, the two syllables and four letters of the word *Deus*:

> How insignificant is this word in its technical dimensions, yet what it expresses could simply not be greater! How is it that this sense, this truth, has entered into your heart? How is it that you know this when you have heard the word, God? How is it that it has entered my heart when I pronounced, 'God'?[17]

A world is overlooked in a word; it simply cannot be contained in its sound. The sound of the word is transcended by the thoughts and emotions it conveys. This holds for all manner of short words, that make their short sounds and then set in motion an infinity of images in the mind and the heart; both in those who speak them and those who hear them. It does not matter. The sounds involve the bodies and hearts of they who speak and those who listen.

The sound grants to thought the certainty of sensible experience. In the formula of Guglielmo di Saint-Thierry: 'Tell it to me, because then I will hear it with the absolute certainty of a sensible experience.'[18] The sounded voice and the interior voice are confounded in this piece of mysticism. On the one hand, it is true that here on earth, we need the proof of 'seeing and touching'. On the other hand, we need these criteria to be the very materialism which the Spirit then overleaps.

The theme of the Divine Voice has another declination, which Augustine will examine in a number of texts, and which poses new and other theological questions in relation to sound. As has already been mentioned, the Father, who creates by medium of an eternal Word independent of sound, nonetheless does express himself in two essential moments in the story of his Son on earth: namely, the Baptism and the Transfiguration.[19] The sonorous and transitory nature of this voice gives rise to questions. For it really does utilize for itself a passing sound, as man talking to man, yet clearly does it never for once cease to be the Voice of the Eternal Father. From the Father in eternity come these words in time, booming forth from a cloud: 'You are my Son, whom I love; with you I am well pleased.'[20] This actual speaking of God in sound sets before us again but differently, the question of the value of the word as a vehicle of understanding thoughts and secrets. The Son does not have anything to learn from his Father: the Son knows everything that the Father knows. The words spoken directly to the Son were therefore in reality spoken indirectly to others (by means of the men at the time, to whom they were spoken directly, in order that these men would hear them and record them). Augustine will mount quite some interrogation of the source of this sound and will arrive at the conclusion – in his reply to the Arians, his *Contra Sermonem Arianorum* – that the Son is the co-producer of the sound.

> In order for these words to pass directly to the Son, they could not be produced without the Son; otherwise, not all the things that were done through Him, could be done through Him.[21]

That is to say, when the Father speaks in sounded Voice, the sound participates in the identity of the substance of the Divine person.

The redemptive octave

In the sounded dimension of the Incarnation, music plays a particular role in bringing us close to the Mystery of it. In Book IV of *De Trinitate*, Augustine describes the purifying and salvific work of Christ that is set into the 'of one, to two' relationship – a relationship that is exhibited and exemplified in music.

> For the death of the sinner springing from the necessity of condemnation is deservedly abolished by the death of the Righteous One springing from the free choice of His compassion, while His single [death and resurrection] answers to our double [death and resurrection]. For this congruity, or suitableness, or concord, or consonance, or whatever more appropriate word there may be, whereby one is [united] to two, is of great weight in all compacting, or better, perhaps, co-adaptation, of the creature. For (as it just occurs to me) what I mean is precisely that co-adaptation which the Greeks call ἁρμονία. However, this is not the place to set forth the power of that consonance of single to double which is found especially in us, and which is naturally so implanted in us (and by whom, except by Him who created us?), that not even the ignorant can fail to perceive it, whether when singing themselves or hearing others. For by this it is that treble and bass voices are in harmony, so that any one who in his note departs from it, offends extremely, not only trained skill, of which the most part of men are devoid, but the very sense of hearing. To demonstrate this, needs no doubt a long discourse; but any one who knows it, may make it plain to the very ear in a rightly ordered monochord.[22]

This analogy drawn between a musical reality and a theological truth does indeed threaten long discourses! However, by the same token, and as Augustine realizes, it also offers a sensational shortcut to its meaning. Because what music does always give us in analogy, is the incontrovertible proof of the senses.

> [*Editor*: It is as close as we can come to the 'seeing is believing' criterion in matters otherwise spiritual and invisible.]

This universality of music can take the place of longer, discursive explanations. Here we come back to a subject familiar to us from the start of this book, namely, the Platonic idea of the universe of number and sound, placed within the soul of man and perceived by him in, and as, the consonance of his soul with what is good and beautiful in and around him.[23] It is in nature that man gets to appreciate the octave, the concordance of extreme sounds, the concordance of the acute with the grave – the image of re-established union between Heaven and earth. This theme of the union of opposites finds its incarnation in Christ, and its manifestation in music. In his coming to earth, Christ brought back into tune that which by sin had been separated. In his death, he conquered death, and restored the Divine nature of man. The insurmountable distance between man, made of fragile flesh, and God, is surmounted in the Incarnate Word. Through his humanization in humility, God is seen, heard, palpated. From the distance between the acute and the grave, is born Harmony! And so it is that in music, we see plain before us that the octave is also the interval that contains within it all the other consonant intervals. It is the one distance in sound that embraces all the other possible distances.

The relationship between the *Musical Christ* and man – the 'of one, to two' relationship – defines, then, salvation.[24] The death and resurrection of Christ came to pass as it did in order to save man from his double-death: that of the soul in sin and that of the body as the scourge of sin. Christ paid for both by a single death: that is, *he dies only in his flesh*.[25] In this way, for the dual death of the impious soul 'abandoned by God'[26] and the body abandoned by the soul on the threshold of resurrection, Christ offered and took upon himself his unique death and resurrection.

This plan of salvation very clearly gets expressed in sensible experience, if only we let the musical analogy do its work. The musical image encloses within itself the mission of Christ on earth, and does so by means of analogy to *proportion*. The relationship of one to two is the relationship of one to its difference, that is, of itself with, now, the difference made possible by – or in relation to – that *self*. Altogether (excuse the pun!), this is the discovery of a unity in anticipation of the difference that comes together to make it. It is the discovery of a unity that could just as well (in theory) be destroyed by either party in its arrangement, but isn't. Instead, when two notes come together in consonance to make a harmonious union, it is as though they could never have been apart. For Augustine, this is where music and musical analogy do inestimable work for us.

The Word became flesh, and here we see music offering us a sonorous hypostasis of the Incarnate Word: incarnate in order to be touched, audible in order to be heard, visible in order to give testimony to the Invisible. In short, in the historical moment of the Incarnation, hearing and sight contributed equally to our material knowing of the Son. The theophany of sound and song was completed in this opportunity to represent musically, the union of the Incarnate Word with man.

Intoning Head and responding Body

Christ, Head of the Body of the Church, whose unity of members is daily reaffirmed in song, was never more 'in music' than at the moment of his Passion. In the Psalms giving advance announcement of his Passion, some talk of responsorial chant, conferring on it an allegorical sense; other of these Psalms use musical metaphors.

Psalm 87 offers a first-class example of what I mean. Its title, *Pro Melech ad respondendum*, indicates a particular kind of song. *Pro Melech* stands for 'the choir', and the choir are here expected to respond to the singer in consonant manner.[27] (Augustine admits that there might be another possible interpretation of the title, but he does not know it and moreover, he did look in the ancient texts but did not succeed in turning it up.) Augustine's interpretation of Psalm 87 exemplifies how responsorial chant acquires its theological and allegorical dimensions.

From the Psalm, Augustine extrapolates, and begins to populate its choir with tropes drawn from the Evangelists and from the Acts of the Apostles. He recreates the dialogue between the biblical passages surrounding the Passion and incorporates the musical dimension, specifically that of responsorial chant.

> Here is announced the Passion of the Christ. But the apostle Peter says: 'To this you were called, because Christ suffered for you, leaving you an example, that you should follow in his steps.' (1 Peter 2, 21)[28]

From here begin the allegorical readings and the analogy between the responsorial chant and the imitation of the Passion of Christ.

The master of the choir

'The choir represents concord, the fruit of charity.'[29] The voice of the choir is the voice of one who follows in the example of Christ, together with the voice of recognition and of membership in the fraternal concord of followers. This voice, and this imitation, would not be possible without love. Augustine pushes this logic so far as to flatly disqualify the choir-song in the case of those who do not imitate with love, or for love.[30] Again, as in his commentary on Psalm 72, at the heart of the Christian message and in the duty of the faithful, love and song are interdependent in a most vital way. To this end, Augustine recounts some musical terminology:

> Further, as in Latin the terms Precentor and Succentor are used to denote in music the performer who sings the first part, and him who takes it up; just so in this song of the Passion, Christ going before is followed by the choir of martyrs unto the end of gaining crowns in Heaven.[31]

The metaphor of the *Musical Christ* is thus preceded by the analogy drawn from the way the Psalm is sung; the way itself in its form and order announcing the Passion and then being the Passion.

Christ in his Passion becomes the Master of the choir. He becomes the Voice Who intones, and which is followed by the choir of martyrs in stark imitation of him. This Christ appears in three guises: (1) as announced in the Psalms, (2) as present at the Incarnation and (3) as suffering in his Passion. 'We listen, therefore, to the Voice of Christ that sings first in prophecy. We respond to him as his choir, imitating and rendering him thanks.'[32] In this way, Augustine closes his introduction to the Psalm and initiates his commentary on it.

The analogies between the song of Christ and the moment of his Passion are developed in the course of the commentary. Christ incites his disciples to support him in his suffering as the choir are invited to respond to his song.[33] The responsorial chant seems to be an ideal model because the cantor/faithful can really and practically complete the imitation of Christ in song. The sung form unites this imitation with the harmony of the one with the other. The responsorial chant becomes thus the mirror to the basic request made to all Christians: to imitate Christ with the same love that Christ has loved us.

In similar manner is the union of the Body with the Head translated in music. As in his commentary on verse 5 of Psalm 42, Augustine interprets the Evangelical passage: 'My soul is overwhelmed with sorrow to the point of death.'[34] It is one of the passages most often interpreted by him in these situations. He sees that in each moment that the suffering of the body is inevitable, there proceeds the sadness that is really a pain in soul.[35] By assuming the human form unto death, Christ suffered, accepting voluntarily the consequences of human weakness.

> These sufferings should not be thought of as sin, but as the just results of human frailty. And so, just as the choir that sings in harmony with the voice that precedes it, his body was able to learn how to suffer for its Head.[36]

The image of responsorial chant transforms Christ into a Musical Man, such that the Church and the faithful may model themselves upon him. Choir and body stand in for each other to make the analogy. In this way, as the body/choir sings in harmony with the soul/Intoner, so does the Body suffer and act in a manner consonant with the Head.

The soul and the body of Christ, united in the suffering of the Passion, are duplicated in the Head (Christ) and the Body (the Church and the faithful). The second learns how to suffer by following the first, and both are mirrored in the musical analogy of the Maestro and the choir. The choir-body follows that which is said by the voice of the Intoner-Soul and the *Musical Christ*, Maestro of the choir, asks of the musical men that they imitate him unto the suffering of his soul and his body.

'The form of the voice'

The words of the Evangelist as to Christ being sad unto death re-invoke in Augustine's commentary the role of listening and place once again 'voice' at the centre of debate. Christ was sad, he was afraid and he shook. But, 'not in himself but in us was he afraid.'[37] That is, in his human nature was he afraid, not in his Divine nature, which was in fact rejoicing in its future resurrection. The being 'in us' implies once again that we must think of language and reciprocity: '[God] did not disdain to transfigure us in him and to speak in our language, so that we might be able to speak in his.'[38] Not only did God make sounds in order to be heard, but so that man might speak with Divine words: the transformation was accomplished through the Word made flesh, so that Divinity might be returned to man, and put back in him. The Christian message of the old man transformed into the New, of death swallowed up in victory, is communicated to man through the Word. God has assumed human words so that man might speak Divinely afterwards.

In the moment of the Passion, there echo also other human words, mirroring the sadness of soul. Christ assumes the voice of the Body when he cries: 'My God, my God, why have you forsaken me?'[39] As Augustine will stress on a number of occasions in his commentaries, this was the voice of human weakness, of our weakness.[40] At the apex of his Passion, Christ pronounced these words in his compassion for men, rather than in his majesty.[41] The Father had never abandoned the Son, but the Son had assumed the nature of the flesh, and therefore *the form of the voice* of the flesh (*similitudinem vocis*). God had expressed himself in the voice of men, for men,[42] so that man might find within himself the same cry, and the same voice.[43] Likewise, 'We were in him when he said, "Sad is my soul unto death."'[44] Therefore, it was for men that Christ prayed before his Passion and cried out to his Father in human voice.[45] And it is to this voice now that the cries and prayers and exultations of man, in tears and in song, make echo. Man sings for the future, and prays in the here and now. Sings for that which he hopes, and cries for the present.[46]

Again, it is a prayer of Christ made audible to man *expressly* so that man might know how to prayer himself.[47] Man responds with a human prayer, pronounced in the secret place of his conscience: 'Where God sees, where God listens.'[48] We say then that the prayer of the Son testifies both to the difference and the similarity between the Voice of the Intoner – of the Maestro – and that of the choir. Between the Voice of the God-Man and the voice of man himself, in prayer.

Christ, in Whom the Word does not prayer but is heard abroad; and which does not ask for help, but, together with the Father, gives succour to all.[49]

This prayer competes, then, both for the man and for the Son. When Jesus prayers, he expresses his human nature, but in words that are always performative.

My prayer – so to say – was returning into my chest.[50]

This was because being the Son, but separated from the Father, he prayed in a way that no man could. That is, he prayed in order to remember the presence of the *Father within Him*.
This is how Augustine would like us to speculate upon voice and word in this passage from the Evangelist. It makes for the theological weft of the Psalms of the Passion. The responsorial chant carries within it a rich symbolism that confers to the chant its extra-musical dimension. The imitation of Christ, and the 'similarity of difference' between the Voice of Christ in this moment and the voice of man, takes us to places that are equally musical and theological. In these places, are born the relationships of Head and Body, the metaphor of the *Musical Christ* and of the man of music who follows him – who follows him in the Passion, the Last Prayer, in Confession and in Invocation.
As we have seen here, the musical form of responsorial chant allows for much interpretation. From the trope, or motif, of the text to the allegory of the Celestial-Intoner-made-Man. In the second type of passionate Psalm, the type we shall next consider, Augustine no longer develops the musical form in its theological analogies, but thinks of and represents Christ and the symbols of the Passion in analogy with various musical instruments.

The wood of the cross: Musical instrument of glory resounding

Already in the Pythagorean, Platonic and Aristotelian texts, music was transforming anger, pain, sadness and depression into their opposites. The passions of the soul were said to be placated by the performative and freeing power of music. In Christian thought, if the praises on the harp shaped the musician in the image of the Creator, then music elevated the spirit and cured the suffering passions of the soul by bringing them into accord with the well-ordered rhythms of music. These passions speak their suffering, while this suffering asks for liberation. This liberation would be a return to a state of harmony. The Passion of Christ speaks exactly of this; and not by chance, then, that Augustine's commentaries bring on to the scene many musical instruments.

The 'timbral of the cross'

The commentary on Psalm 33 offers a synthesis of the musical metaphors of the Passion. From the beginning of his interpretation of this Psalm, in which David plays his timbral at the gates of the city, Augustine records the promise in Scripture that if you ask, the door shall be opened to you.[51] Inspired by this, he pushes on with a Christological interpretation of this Davidic Psalm. David, who, according to the title of the Psalm, 'changed his countenance before Alimech and sent him away', represents Christ who changed his sublimity in humility before changing death into life. In the Passion, Christ changed his countenance in the presence of the Jews, in the same way that David changed his: 'he was full of affection ... and drummed his timbral before the gates of the city.' David was mad with affection. Just as Christ was in his compassion for humanity. This was the compassion of one who, for love, suffers together with men, and who leads them to his Passion in order to signal to them the end of suffering. We see here, then, the beginnings of a new link between love and music.

'Where there is affection, there is mercy.'[52] The compassion of the heart walks in step with affection, leaving it that there is no space in between for judging the other, but for suffering together with him in full comprehension of his state. In compassion, it is impossible not to put oneself in the other's shoes and to share, as much as one can, in their passion. It is for this, that affection always transforms the countenance. It was in this way that David was mad with affection while he drummed before the gates of the city; and why he changed his countenance.

What then is, 'He affected?' He was full of affection. For what is so full of affection as the Mercy of our Lord Jesus Christ, who, seeing our infirmity, that He might deliver us from everlasting death, underwent temporal death with such great injury and contumely? And He drummed: because a drum is not made, except when a skin is extended on wood; and David drummed, to signify that Christ should be crucified.[53]

As in Augustine's commentary on Psalm 32, here organology directs the metaphor. The symbolic significance of the musical instrument must be uncovered by examination of its exact technical parameters. The analogy between the stretched leather on the wood of the instrument and the stretched skin of Christ on the cross goes beyond this material equivalence to show us a similarity of affection between the two instruments (the timbral and the cross). David, by drumming, 'showed affection' and opened the gates of the city in a way that should remind us of how the hard hearts of men, hitherto closed to Christ and his suffering, were opened 'by the timbral of the cross'.[54] Here, the affective power of music along with its performative dimension is confounded with the same affective power and the same performative dimension in the words of Christ and in his death on the cross for the salvation of men. Developing the analogy, Augustine creates the concept of the 'timbral of the cross (*tymphano crucis*)',[55] identifying the musical instrument with the instrument of the Passion, and making both into a single instrument, and a single meaning.

To 'drum on the timbral' becomes the same thing as to 'die on the cross'. If to play on the harp was in addition to man fulfilling the Law (the expression, in joy, of fulfilling it), for the Son, 'to play' *was* 'to die' and therefore *was* the exact same thing as fulfilling the Will of the Father (the Son did not descend from the cross[56]). In the identification between drumming on the timbral and dying on the cross, the musical analogy shows its conceptual power, in the way that it brings us to unite the Old and New Testaments. David played in order that Christ might be crucified. And in order to understand this image, Augustine will use a physical description of the process:

> Because He Who was crucified was stretched out on the wood, in the same way that, to make a timbral, the flesh, or the skin, must

be stretched out over the wood, it was said: 'and he drummed on the timbral', that is, that He was crucified, that he was stretched out on the wood.[57]

In this way, we arrive at the union of the Two Testaments by way of a musical image! 'With the cross, was opened the hearts of mortals, that is, the timbral was drummed.'[58] The cross also becomes the synonym for the 'key': both the key that opens and the musical key that tunes and renders harmonious. Centuries later, Bonaventura would develop this idea. In the Passion, Christ was transformed into a musical instrument: the tuning keys were the nails fixed through his hands, while to the wood of the cross and over Christ's body were strung the seven strings of the instrument, and, as we have already mentioned, each of them can be seen as representing one each of Christ's last words.[59] In fact, the cross-musical key idea leads to another interpretation, in which Augustine comments on the biblical recommendation 'To celebrate the Saviour with the chitara: to celebrate the Saviour, by offering him your bodies as a living sacrifice.'[60] If the body is here represented by the musical instrument, in imitation of the *Musical Christ* on the cross, then the faithful work by playing with love, to the end of transforming their suffering passions into a fitting harmony.

Again, the plan of salvation is contained in the musical image. The key, the wood, the stretched-out skin and the sound which manifests affection are all of them notions that Augustine transfers from the musical instrument to the Passion. The tuning key opens the door to harmony and opens wide the hearts of men, in the same way that the timbral drummed upon by David pre-announced the promise of freedom of the cross of Christ.

The musical confession

The glory of Christ in extreme humility is repeated in the song of man, both in the present, in confession and conversion, and in the future: 'in my humility I shed tears for you, I will sing my glory to you.'[61] Christ, plus the cross transformed into the glorious musical instrument of David, indicates the union of humility and glory and allows that the imitation of the humility of Christ on the part of the faithful actually transforms their words into glorious words.

The human words are seen to reach for this glory, because they are humble and naked in their confession. These glorious words of man are those that he speaks into the ear of God because they are on his heart.[62]

There is, then, in man, a Divine listening, which – as it were – 'listens in' on the intimate (baggage of his heart) as it lowers itself into the ear of God. The 'ear of God'[63] will come to be defined many times by Augustine. In short, it is the operative incorporeal presence of which we have – in the 'ear of God' – the sensible image. The ear of God stands for a fulfilling kind of listening. It fulfils the man who is capable of it. In fact, we say that the incorporeal members of God are visible in man, and that in this case, then, the material ear of man comes to be seen in its incorporeal, Godly power (of fulfilling listening). The human ear is transformed into an interior ear, that, like the Divine listening, 'meets [hears] the needs of the heart, and not the spoken voice'.[64]

In another commentary, in response to the same question – what is intended in the expression 'ear of God'? – Augustine suggests that the Son becomes the ear of the Father.[65] God inclines his ear to man: 'This God did when he sent Christ to us.'[66] God inclined himself by incarnating himself; and his ear, now a synecdoche of Christ, was exalted as the place of truth. In this way, the lowering of Heaven to earth is able to include love and truth in the metaphor of the ear and listening. Listening is presented now as the place of love and therefore of truth, and so gives to Augustine the opportunity – as in his commentary on Psalm 9 – to reaffirm the immateriality of the ear of God. Thus, it is incorporeal because 'the truth is neither square, nor round, nor long'.[67] The ear of God listens to the interiority of Being, and invites the latter to listen, too: 'Truth is never reached by those who seek it outside themselves.'[68] 'It is everywhere present, if the eye of the heart can only be open to it.'[69] The truth offers itself to the eye of the heart that is open to hear it. The Divine ear is therefore none other than this place of interior listening, and is recognized for what it is insofar – only insofar – as it permits knowledge of itself and reciprocates with it. In all, and for all of this, listening becomes love. 'God inclined his ear to us, making to flow over us his love.'[70]

The confession of the truth of the heart resounds in the spiritual and silent voice of the soul. It does not move the material air,[71] but proceeds from the intimate recess of the heart and requests the

Divine listening.[72] It is not solely audible to the Invisible, but may be heard by those who incline the ears of their hearts.[73] The Divine ear is also present in every instance in which one person succeeds in comprehending another in their silence. 'Hear my cry,' demands the intelligible music of the soul. And, in the Augustinian imagination, man can indeed intone the music of his heart and elevate himself to the Divine hearing; but on condition always, that he succeeds in being truly consoled.[74]

[*Editor:* This 'condition' is, I think, one of the more daring demands, or dynamics, of Augustine's mature thought; but especially of his Christology. It can be very hard to take, especially if one's formal, doctrinal instruction in the Christian God has focused on his majesty, on man's pitiful, sinful state in relation to it, and therefore on the absolute all-importance of the membership of the Church, understood as the body of the faithful with Christ as its Head. As we have seen in this book, Augustine can be cited as having made the signal contribution to all of this; as indeed he did. However, there is a whole other side to Augustine's thought, which runs concurrently with his doctrinal orthodoxy and supports it, but which operates from out of the free open spaces of the 'other side'. If it helps, we can see Laurence's book as working in this place of the other side. Music has long – that is, from before Christian times – been the special language of this place. Laurence's book has shown us why. In this free open space of the other side, there are no articles of faith which must be defended at all costs. There is therefore no 'truth', as wearing some uniform which would identify it to us. There is just body and soul, matter and spirit – Plus the curious ways in which they prove each other. We have already encountered, through Augustine and Laurence, the *Octave*, and the inexplicability of it. (We are its proof each time.) To Augustine, this means that we own a point of view that matters. And to Augustine, this was demonstrated in the ease with which God was made Man. So easily, and so naturally, in fact, was he made Man, that by the majority he was unrecognized as God unto death on the cross. This is a very big, but very uncharted fact. Again, to Augustine, it means we own a point of view that matters. Christ's crucifixion on the cross is what it is because we can put ourselves in his place, and feel his every pain and desperation, and cry out to our

Father in Heaven. Augustine would use this all the time, but most of all when he was making his special music in the Psalms. This music is what it is because God really does speak in a language that we can understand, and we in a language that he can understand. There is a shared affection between us and him, that has never been lost. To return to the start of this reflection, in the traditional picture of the original sin, in which we turned from God in order to strike out on our own in pride, this point can get lost; as in, 'out with the bathwater'. But even if the Devil knows and can remember the sound of God's Voice, then so can we still now, by half. What was so abominable and inexcusable in the original sin, was that we turned from God freely and willingly – Knowing exactly what it was that we were turning from, and turning nonetheless. This earned us damnation, and earned it fairly. Had we turned instead in some fit of pique, or in some way deluded and not in our right minds, then God might well have shown his mercy upon us there and then; and in fact we would not then be talking of the 'original sin' but of something childish and instantly forgivable. So, to recap, in spite of the fire and brimstone of original sin, there is something we have never lost. The Apostle called it the 'Law of the Heart' (also known as the 'Perfect Law of Liberty' or simply (and as we have encountered it in this book) the 'Law of Love'). Christian apologists down the centuries – but especially those in the modern age who have attempted to resist the human creation of new ethics based in scientific, or biological imperatives – have called it by the 'Lights of Conscience' or the 'Moral Law'. Augustine's line, laid down in his own life's experience as recounted in his *Confessions*, is that the human heart is in a state of dynamic equivalence with God. That is to say, the presence of God to someone is the same thing as the heart in them that feels it. Again, this is really just another way of saying that the human heart can never be mistaken in this matter. Or again, that it is in effect birthed into life each time by grace (from scratch, so to speak) in order to receive into it the presence of God. This intrinsic debt to the supernatural, which finds its perfect analogy in music and its affect, but yet which has been side-lined for a century according to the historical methods of modern musicology, is what I take Paolo Gozza to mean in his Preface when he observes that we have lost contact with the nature and function of 'music's image'.]

When God lends us his ear and hears the voice of our heart, he offers also his presence.[75] In the same way, can another human being make themselves present in the confessor's heart, and (supernaturally, by grace) hear him aright. 'He who has the ear of my heart, there where I am.'[76] This other can then hear the voice of confession in the heart – 'the interior mouth',[77] the place of repose – before it has been uttered in sound.

In confession, the (human) song returns to the shape of the final confession of the Son that goes, 'I will confess You in eternity. I hear the voice of your Firstborn, about to die for me, who says, "Unto you, O Lord, I will cry"'.[78] At the heart of this cry launched into eternity by the Man-made-God, at the heart of this cry made musical by its representation in imagery by the human musical instruments and their song, is seen and fulfilled the *transformation*.

> You have changed my cry into joy, because I sang my glory to you and was not sad, because I no longer shed tears but sang to you, not in humility, but in my glory, insofar as you have raised me from my humility.[79]

On the cross, in the ultimate act of humility, Christ drew men to him and then raised them with him from the condition of mortality to life eternal. The (responsorial) chant has the function of expressing this attraction that raised by changing the cry into relief. In the place of the cry that impedes words is substituted the chant that responds to the harmony between Heaven and earth in the hour of the Passion.

The theme of Christ the musical instrument on the cross, or the *Musical Christ*, is therefore interpreted together with the theme of the Divine listening and, complementary to this theme, confession. In the weakness of suffering and in the humility of confession, man is elevated to glorious song, as Christ from the cross was able to raise man to bring him up to glory. The ear of God is the place of hearing and of hospitality, of compassion and of Grace. It is the place of truth, the synecdoche of Christ and the action of the Father. It hears every word made musical on the model of the confession of the Son who for love, conceded unto death. Christ confesses to the Father by playing upon the chitara of his dying body, and in death he delivers to man the song of glory, in order that it might be expressed by man here, and now, in each and every time that he confesses his love.

Risen body, and body of sound

In suffering, in love, in resurrection, the body is always present and the analogy that Augustine makes between the musical instrument and bodily actions holds as well for the sons of God (men) as for the works of the Son of God. In this sense, Augustine returns to the images of the chitara and the harp pursued in his commentary on Psalm 56 and gives them a Christological interpretation. The Passion comes to be thought of in another musical image, complementing this one (of the chitara and harp), and in which now Glory is identified with the musical instruments.

Verse 9 of Psalm 56 – 'Awake, my soul! Awake, harp and chitara!' – is the invitation to Augustine to develop his allegory of the musical instruments.[80] The first contradiction which appears to meet him, and which he must then 'melt', as per his technique, is the mentioning of two instruments as against just the one body of the risen Christ. As in other commentaries, Augustine will solve this in organology. Thus, the chitara and the harp will become for him *organa*, which will put them into their generic status as 'instruments serving to accompany song'. This will be done to differentiate them in a category as against the organ (*organum* – 'that big instrument which you blow with bellows'[81]). Now, with this sorting done, *organa* can stand for a (single) class of corporeal musical instruments, albeit with the critical distinction still holding between the chitara and the harp as regards the relative positions of their sound boxes – the harp's up above, and the chitara's down below; as we saw in Augustine's commentary on Psalm 32.

'It came to pass that Christ played upon his harp and his chitara, and said: "I will rise on the good morning."'[82] (He was risen on the stroke of morning; see Mark 16, 2.) Just as in the commentary on Psalm 32, the harp and the chitara symbolized the two types of human action, so here do they do the same in reference to the actions of the *Musical Christ*. 'It came to pass that Christ played': that is, that he *worked*; because to play, is the work of two hands. If in reference to man, the harp stood for the works done according to the Law and the chitara to those done in tribulation, in Christ, the harp stands now for miracles, while the chitara stands for the Passion. 'By means of his flesh, Christ fulfilled two types of action: miracles and the Passion.'[83] As the sound arrives from the sound box that sits in the high part of the harp, so are miracles generated from on high by means of the body (miracles make use of the natural, albeit in stupefying arrangements). The body of Christ in the fulfilment of miracles is therefore the mirror of the body of the harp.

'The flesh insofar as it completes Divine works is the harp; the same flesh, insofar as it supports the miseries of human life, is the chitara.'[84] One cannot do without the body: the body resounds in joy, in miracles and every time that its possessing being works actions that are suited to its soul. Likewise, it resounds in woe when its being – whether the Son, or plain man – supports its sufferings and hears its soul crying out in dissonance against them. Miracles and miseries, harp and chitara: the body is always engaged in action. In the *Musical Christ* metaphor, musical sound acquires a miraculous performative power: 'Play on the harp: the blind will be illuminated, the deaf will hear, the paralytics will find their strength, the lame will walk, the sick will be healed and the dead will rise. This is the sound of the harp.'[85] What we see here is that action is always a function of body, and that the body resounds in sound. This is the *sound* of the harp. To play the harp becomes synonymous with the action performed upon the bodies in their ailments – blindness, deafness – while to play the chitara is to suffer by having assumed this same body (in the first place).

'He also played the chitara: when he was hungry, thirsty, slept, was captured, whipped, derided, crucified, buried.'[86] The Christ who 'was hungry, thirsty, slept', in other words, who suffered unto death on the cross for the salvation of men is therefore a Christ who is playing upon the chitara. The action of the body is identified with the acting power of glorious or suffering sound. It is in sound that Christ was hungry up to the time that he was buried, in sound that he gave sight to the blind and resuscitated the dead. And in sound that he rose again. In this way, we see how is resolved the seeming paradox of having two musical images for Christ's one body.

> 'When, therefore, you see in that flesh something played from on high and something from below, while one is the flesh that is risen, then we recognise in the one and the same flesh the harp and the chitara.'[87]

The miracles and the Passion – the two forms of action and their sonorous images – are both the work of the body of Christ as musical man.

We see that the material, qualitative, organological and formal dimensions of music come together to give a musical image of Christ. The *Musical Christ*: the voice of the Celestial Intoner who leads the choir of the faithful: the timbral made from skin stretched over the wood of salvation: or the harp of chords resounding in the hearts of its hearers. And now one more! *Silence*!

The silence of the Passion

The silence of Christ in the moment of his arrest is often commented upon by Augustine. Sometimes this takes the form of a typology of the silence of man (in general), at other times in comparison with the silence imposed upon the musical instruments in Psalm 136.

Sing the words of silence

One of the meanings of the silence of Christ in the Passion can be found in Augustine's commentary on Psalm 7. There, he interweaves silence, the word and the song. The war conducted against David by his son Absalom, in league with David's former servant Hushai (Chusi), whose name means *silence*, and with Absalom being advised by Ahithophel, whose name mean's 'brother's ruin' (*Fratris ruina*), is interpreted by Augustine in a Christological key. Ahithophel prefigures Judas and Hushai the silence of Christ at the moment of his arrest. In this context, the silence becomes a synonym for 'secret': Christ 'contended against that guile in high silence, that is, in that most deep secret, whereby blindness happened in part to Israel (See Rom. 11, 25)'.[88] This 'most deep secret' and 'high silence' testify better than any word to the mystery of the 'ways of Wisdom'.[89] Being lets itself be guided by these mysterious ways, understood from the heart that is ignored by the outside world. It does not respond to the accusations of men. It follows the silence of Christ.

Christ did not retort when he was accused of being demoniac. He did not say that the Devil was in those who were speaking. 'He did not say this, even though he would have spoken truly had he said it, for it was simply not the moment to say it.'[90] Truly did Christ prefer not to speak then. He 'ignored what he had heard.'[91] 'As if he had not heard it.'[92] Because he knew not to respond. 'It was necessary to remain silent in the Passion, He Who would not be silent in judgement!'[93] We say that this dichotomy of sound – of silence and words – contained the Divine plan unto Universal Judgement.

Christ was silent in the face of his nemesis because he knew that he must not speak. For if he did, he would not be (properly) understood. This silence is thus the sign of wisdom and yet, in its polysemy, in other contexts, the absence of sound is also darkness.[94] 'Sound is rhythm's light (illumination), in the same way as silence is as darkness compared to colours.'[95] In this scheme, silence stands to sound in the same way that darkness stands to light: while darkness is to hate what light is to love.[96] In other words, darkness 'blinds': the absence of light – that is, the presence of hate, anger, jealousy, ignorance – covers the truth of things and makes it that one does not know how to see that truth. Clearly, this is not what we are talking of here! Therefore, it is a sign that we must interpret the silence of Christ through our interior vision. For again: Christ 'did not reveal it, explaining it rather in his great silence and showing it to us in our admiration.'[97] That is to say, what should interpret the silence for us is the sheer gesture of it, not the discourse of it. Christ *showed* the silence: in leaving himself to be arrested, he showed the significance of a silence comprehensible only to the as yet indecipherable plan of salvation.

In this way, silence hides and protects *The Mystery*. It keeps concealed the mystery of the Passion even while it converts the words of the traitor into salvation. And whoever enters into the heart of the mystery having (thus) heard the silence can sing. The song of David's Psalm is reserved for those who have grasped how to decipher what the silence shows.

> The perfect soul then, which is already worthy to know the secret of God, sings a Psalm unto the Lord. She sings for the words of Hushai (Chusi), because she has attained to know the words of that silence.[98]

The persecutors, blinded by ignorant hate, did not understand the words of silence, while 'among Christ's friends there was not silence, but the words of silence, that is the clarity and manifest significance of that silence.'⁹⁹ These 'words of silence' resounded in their clarity.

If silence becomes a manner of speaking reserved for intimates and disciples, then understanding it also becomes the condition of our being able to sing. As if the wise song could ever have been the fitting response to the animal song and signal that made Peter come to understand his denial (his silence). The instant of comprehension does not translate itself in words, but in song or in tears. Yet again does music unite itself to tears. Peter wept bitterly after he came to understand: he wept bitterly after the rooster had sung for the third time.

Both song and tears carry us to an interior comprehension of things. In fact, Augustine really hopes that the words of his commentary will vacate the page so that their place be taken up, instead, by the tears of his reader. If only the words that we have sung and heard, 'might be explained in tears!'[100] We note how words are to be explained by tears, and not the other way around. Because when one weeps, one understands in another way. This new way is no longer rational comprehension, but a comprehension that convenes with things intimate, with things sacred and mysterious, with joy and with sadness. And, in the topography of the Augustinian soul, tears hold a special relationship to song. Each by turn calls on the involvement of the entire person and requires a particular listening. Therefore, Augustine asks: 'that we listen to that which we sing by crying.'[101] The musical sound and the significance of the word reach the one the ear, the other the mind; while both make their way towards the heart. This is an Augustinian theme par excellence as well as a theme par excellence of mysticism.

If the heart that is animated by love cannot be silent, then its words may not always be pronounced. On the model of Christ, man too must know when to be quiet. There is a time for silence, and a time for speaking. In his goodbye to his disciples, Jesus kept some things secret because it was not the time to reveal them; and then in his arrest, he was silent. In his commentary on Psalm 38, Augustine develops the distinction between a convenient quiet and one that is out of turn; and does so no longer in the case of Christ but in the case of man. 'For we cannot help speaking about what we have seen and heard.'[102] This refers to how man cannot be silent concerning that which he has seen by the eye of the heart and heard in his interior ear. Then he hears the voice of the rivers:[103] 'Not only did they speak but they spoke at the tops of their voices.'[104] That is, they spoke in words inspired by God and heard inside them, there where man 'hears something good and true'.[105] To be silent in the face of all of this would be 'out of turn'. Verse 3 of Psalm 38 – 'But when I was silent and still, not even saying anything good' – gives, on the other hand, the criterion of convenient, or as we can now see it, suitable silence. That is, when one is short of anything good to say, when the true listening has not preceded the spoken word, adds Augustine, or simply when the time has come to remain in silence for the sake of hearing truly what is the Divine will in the case.[106] Man therefore finds himself always in this catch between speaking and silence,[107] and this holds also for the musical instruments, in one moment played, in another moment 'hung on the poplars'.

'We hung our musical instruments on the poplar trees'

By the rivers of Babylon we sat and wept
When we remembered Zion.
There on the poplars
We hung our harps,
For there our captors asked us for songs,
Our tormentors demanded songs of joy; they said, 'Sing us one of the songs of Zion!'[108]

Psalm 136 enriches the theme of Christian silence with the hermeneutic of silence as imposed upon the musical instruments. The Augustinian commentary on Psalm 136 gives a symbolic interpretation of the instruments hung on the poplars and of the hymn of praise. The musical instruments are transformed into a musical image that reaches far outside itself and which is charged with an allegorical value rich in significance. In fact, here again the image becomes a symbol thanks to the plurality of extra-musical elements it contains. Zion, synonym of Jerusalem, is the city that aspires to peace eternal and its citizens are the angels, together with those who express the desire of peace through song and action.[109] Different Psalms sing and evoke the name of this city from which the Christians are exiled until they reach it on high, there where reigns an 'ineffable quiet [that] eyes do not see nor ears hear'.[110] One sighs on earth in desire for this quiet and therefore one sings: 'We sing to animate ourselves in desire.'[111]

One sings to give life to desire! In his commentary, Augustine pushes the parallel as far as assimilating desire in song: 'Whoever desires, even if they are silent on the tongue, sings in their heart. On the other hand, whoever does not desire, even if he verily wounds the ears of those around him with his cries, are mute to God.'[112] The desire of the heart is the secret word proffered to the Divine ear who is pleased by the songs of love. Whoever does not desire has not first received from God what is required to fill the heart; and therefore it matters not that he speaks, prays, invokes, cries; for it is all in vain. Augustine can often be seen working the idea of listening, speaking or singing *with heart* – the organ that never sleeps and which pulses in order to give life to the other organs. In this, we are reminded of what Augustine says in his commentary on Psalm 37 of the frost of love in the heart that is silent and, by contrast, the warmth of the continuous voice of he who loves and cannot be silent. In this transport, in this desire of the heart, in this desire of peace, there is always at work the inspiring love of singing. The song is therefore the movement of desire and desire is always caused by the song of the heart. We will return to the expression 'song of the heart' in the last part of our journey in this book.

The citizens of Jerusalem are those who sing and intone on the musical instruments: thus opens Augustine's commentary on the second verse of Psalm 136: 'There on the poplars / We hung our harps'. Augustine offers a theological explanation of the Psalmodic image of the musical instruments hung on the poplars and allows it to be seen how music might here be understood as the emblem of the Christian. In fact, in the commentary, these same musical instruments will go on to become representations of the Scriptures, of the commandments, of the promises of God and of meditations on the life to come.[113]

In all of this, the qualitative dimension of music and instrumental sound find a new and fundamental importance for Augustine. The musical sound comes to indicate the sweetness of Scripture, of Holy promises and of Holy meditations. Those who desire the vision of peace, and who actuate it in pacific meditations, may already be considered to live in Jerusalem even though they still exile in Babylon. (The city where resound the voices of the harpists and musicians, the flautists and trumpet players,[114] who at the end of time will be quieted, as announced in Revelation.) These play the musical instruments described in Psalm 136 every time that they make resound their pacific works. Those however who live in Babylon, but live willingly there, are said to take pleasure in ephemeral goods and do not play their instruments but hang them on the poplars.[115]

To hang the musical instruments on the poplars: Augustine interprets every term (as we have observed before), melting the sense to reach the symbol enclosed within the musical metaphor. The poplars are trees that do not produce fruit; likewise, then, those who do not look to the inside of things come to be nourished on sterile food: 'they cannot think anything of value' and do not desire the vision of peace.[116] They do not hear, and it is not worth the trouble to speak with them, because nothing you could say would go home with them. 'Anything you might say to them, they hear in ways distorted and averse.'[117] The word and the use of Scripture are held back from such and the musical instruments are hung because these people 'cannot carry them'.[118] Moreover, the musical instruments are not said to be tied or placed in the poplars but 'hung'. The use of this generic term instead of a form of binding or placement that might carry additional meaning is to indicate that meaning is only to be attached to the times when they are, or are not to be played. Again, what is to be interpreted is only when, or when not they are to be hung or taken up.[119] In the same way Christ, in speaking his goodbye to his disciples, held back on the things that would need to wait on the Holy Spirit to come: 'I have much more to say to you, more than you can now bear.'[120] Likewise did he remain silent before his nemesis on the night of his arrest, for the justice of his words would not have been understood.

A multiplicity of Augustinian musical themes can be found in the metaphor of the instruments hanging in the trees and waiting to be played: listening, sound and the capacity to make music return here to feature integrally in the musical image. Also, in this musical metaphor of Psalm 136, music as the image of Scripture and of the Word shows us the special place of musical language. Music that does not betray the affect conveyed in poetic texts becomes the allegory of Scripture and of the truth of the Word. And we have seen also how according to the circumstances, it might need to hold itself and remain silent, in the image of the wise silence of he who knows when he must remainder the use of words; as does the musician, when he knows instinctively to introduce a musical pause into his flow.

The musical instrument symbolizes the word of truth and the incapacity of he who listens in an adverse way to share in the truth of the other. It testifies to the truth insofar as it becomes the symbol of sacred Scripture and of the meditated upon promise of life eternal; while on the human level, it allegorizes the other situation, in which the truth meets with ears which do not hear it. Those who do not hear it, we say are full of their own truth which renders them hermetic (impervious) to any other lived truth.

That which resounds among the inhabitants of Babylon is not just materialism, but discord. Those who play well, patiently construct by actuating the Law of Love in musical sound. Those who alter this sound by means of a dissonant listening destroy the heard Word. In this way, music allegorizes the truth of experience, the construction of the Law of Love, the meditation on the eternal and the moment of waiting upon the suspension of the Word. The musical metaphor condenses the Christian message by speaking in a single image of the Word, the hearing of it aright and the Law of Love.

Adverse listening is identified in the remaining verse of Psalm 136 with diabolical listening – the Devil divides, sows discord, listens falsely and destroys ever pacific construction. The Devil is not content merely with not hearing, but calls for his own song. His ministers, entering into men, serve as the tongues of their prisoners and produce by them a song.[121] To the musical instruments as symbols of lived truth is counterposed now this song, such that the sweet sound of the New Law is contrasted with the demand of the Prince of the powers of the air. Here Augustine unifies listening and song: namely, the disposition of the listener with the diabolical deceiver of song. In his commentary he interweaves two levels of reading: one theological, in which the musical metaphors sustain the Christian truth, and one anthropological, in which the same metaphors conduct an investigation of the human psyche.

The disposition of the listener as an indispensable condition of understanding what has been heard passes from the reception of the revealed truths of Christianity to the truth revealed of another. Here is introduced again the idea of distorted listening, but this time on the basis of being overfilled with proper sounds: 'You must empty yourself of that which you now hope to receive.'[122] In practice, this means emptying oneself of preconceived ideas in order to draw close to the thoughts of the other.

False listening hangs on the requests of the tormentors who say, 'Sing us one of the songs of Zion!' In these words, we hear others; at least, Augustine intends us to hear them: 'They ask us to explain to them why Christ was come and what is this other life, because they are not disposed to believe it. They ask us to explain to them why they should believe.'[123] 'Sing us' becomes the equivalent of 'Explain to us', in the way of association between *singing* and *explaining* and *comprehending* that you find often at the start of Augustine's commentaries on the Psalms. Usually, the parallel is made between the act of singing the Psalm and its comprehension. In singing, the significance of the text is melted; in that expression we have been so fond of using in this book. However, in the context of what we have been saying here on 'deaf ears' and 'overstuffed' minds, someone standing in need of an explicating song is likely not predisposed to believe in the first place. Here, Augustine shows his canny grasp of human nature or human psychology. The problem is pride, or how people are invariably taken up with their own thoughts. 'Even if I could expound the goods of Jerusalem, you could not understand them. For you must first empty yourself of that which presently fills you, in order to be in the position of being filled with that which you so sorely miss.'[124] We lack the space here to make examples also of those who do not know how to listen or play musical instruments (*noli percutere organum ut sonnet*), and those who rattle out questions for the sake of it: 'Speak to me, sing to me, explain to me.'[125] Let us just say that the man like this, 'asks in a misleading way, that is, not to learn but to object. Therefore, I will not speak and I will [instead] hang my musical instruments.'[126] To any who asks merely in order to judge, we do not respond, even if he asks for a song or a hymn. He asks for a song, but with a false disposition of the heart. He does not want to learn but to counter with his own. He does not want to open himself, but to judge, as we said. He does not want to listen to what he has already thrown away!

'Sing us one of the songs of Zion!' To this deceiving request responds a song proffered in the midst of the taunts and false praises. 'In fact, this man who was singing – and this man would be us, if we chose it – had to endure from every side these requests, that were then taken back with taunts.'[127] We see now that Augustine is presenting us here with the model of Christ, in that the man holds back his song in the face of false requests to sing it. Augustine then interprets and integrates the parable of the rich young man, which goes that a rich man comes towards Jesus and asks him what he must do to obtain the eternal life.[128] 'He was interrogating [Jesus] on the eternal life, which we will take here as to be the same as though he were demanding of Jesus one of the Songs of Zion.'[129] The rich young man follows this up by asking which of the commandments he should observe. 'And the Saviour sang him one of the Songs of Zion, knowing full well that the man would not understand it.' Jesus ran the risk of not being understood. In this instance, he does not hold back the Word, even though he knows that the rich young man does not truly wish to know.

In the Augustinian imagination, the responses by Jesus when he does choose to respond – and whether to the questions of those who ask without listening, or to those who ask truly desiring to listen (with love) – are the songs of Christ turned to the *City of Peace*. It is once again the *Musical Christ* who is in these expressing himself, and the musical metaphor demonstrates once again, then, the special place of music in Augustinian thought. Christ not only speaks but sings, even if he is not understood. In singing his response, Christ wants to give an example of how many 'approve only up to the point of our giving them the answer they desire to receive.'[130] If the response does not correspond to the one they wanted to hear, they do not hear it; and starting from this premiss, Augustine develops his idea that the song of eternal life really is simply impossible to sing in a strange land. 'How can we sing the songs of the Lord while in a foreign land?'[131] In the parable of the rich young man, Christ furnishes the example of what ultimately is meant here: yes you can sing to those without ears to hear it, yes you can sing to those inhabited by malicious spirits of disharmony and discord, yes you can sing to the rich man full of his own wisdom, but you will not be heard!

This weaving of the musical metaphors of the Psalm with the Evangelist's words is such that each comes to be included in the other as if in a single passage. Thanks to this interpretative method of Augustine's, the various parts cannot but enrich each other. 'But the one who was saddened left. And we said after him: "How can we sing the songs of the Lord while in a foreign land?" And he went away.'[132] As we can see, then, the parable of the rich young man becomes quite confused with this Psalm, as far as Augustine is concerned. And then another passage from Scripture is brought in, that from Timothy, in which the rich are asked not to be arrogant.[133] This is interpreted to show us that the rich too have received a song of Zion, a Divine Word addressed to them to help them to reach the City of Peace, and that when the Apostle gave this recommendation to them for their salvation, 'he played the musical instruments and did not leave them to hang.'[134]

The Augustinian commentary arrives at a place not reached by the Psalm itself. It teaches that we should (in fact) take up the musical instruments from the poplars, because in Sacred Scripture, various are the examples of how they should be played. The song of Zion given by Timothy to the rich is developed metaphorically: that the rich should not puff themselves up, that they should do the good by giving alms, they should play their musical instruments.[135] On the other hand, faced with those who accuse them of dismantling their true patrimony (and culture), they should waste no time in hanging their instruments on the poplars. 'But beyond these trees, they should not cease to sing, that is to do works of good.'[136] Because, 'just as they have begun to learn how to listen, then can we meet their ears with songs they are now capable of receiving.'[137] The synonymity of *singing*, *playing* and *working* leads Augustine to his big send-off: 'Brothers, your musical instruments must not cease to do good. Sing to each other the songs of Zion.'[138] Finally, those who forget peace are asked not to sing: 'May my tongue cling to the roof of my mouth if I do not remember you.'[139] And it is not enough just to remember this, but it depends upon something over and above the remembering that bears upon it: 'Pay attention to how you remember. Something we remember in hate, some other thing in love.'[140] Every time that man remembers in love, he intones the song of Jerusalem. This is because with love positioned prior to his remembering, that same love actually reaches forwards and modifies the sentiment in his memory, thus bringing about the right song.

The *Musical Christ* who is silent is the wise man who hangs the instruments upon the poplars when it suits him to keep silent while all the other protagonists of the Psalm and the parable – Christ, the Apostle, the rich men – express themselves in music.

This wise silence leads us out to our final and promised destination in this book: the silence of Divine music and of the Song of the Heart: the ultimate and supreme musical concepts for Augustine.

4

The Father

In Christian thought, the musical man is identified with the New Man. Renovated by Grace and by the song of praise, and possessed of a new song, he can hear the music of the Father and is attracted by it to the Father's house. This final chapter of our journey through the figures of the musical man brings us up to the two dimensions of *silent music* according to Augustine. That of the man who sings the ineffable with the voice of his heart and that of *The Ineffable* who sings to the ears of the heart of man.

The spiritual man, defined by Saint Paul in his *First Letter to the Corinthians*, is he who has known the Spirit of God and who therefore speaks with the words that teach of that same Spirit. Better than words, in the Augustinian imagination, the interior man is expressed in the new song – the song of the heart – or, when he overflows in unspeakable joy, in a pure musical sound liberated from words. That which we cannot say in words, but of which we do not wish to remain silent, must be spoken in sound or in silence.

Not only is it not possible to speak in words of the Divine Ineffability, but the experience of beauty is similarly unspeakable. 'Beauty is intimacy,'[1] says Augustine, in lapidary mode. Beauty is always intimate because experience speaks to intimacy and only in intimacy can one make the experience of it. However, verbal language is not adapted to testify to it, because the experience of beauty does not leave itself to be translated, nor reduced, to words.

The ineffable music of the creature

In my opinion, Saint Paul has the way of representing the paradigm of the Ineffable, par excellence. Namely, *Rapt*: 'He heard inexpressible things, things that man is not permitted to tell.'[2] This happens when a man escapes from himself in aesthetic or ecstatic experience, always untellable.[3] In ecstasy – the escape from oneself[4] – Saint Paul is transported towards the things supernal and interior of which he can say nothing.[5] The impossibility of speaking, the loss of words, leads necessarily to silence and this silence is – then – the only word adequate to express in its full amplitude the experience of beauty vouched. And yet there is need still of recounting this beauty (as we are doing here), in order to conserve at least some trace of it.

The sound of the unsayable

In order to testify to beauty, verbal language dissolves itself into song, into sound, into breath, into silence. In his commentary on Psalm 32, Augustine offers a symbolical interpretation of the New Song in order to then – as in other commentaries – define jubilation in relationship to song and to *pure sound*.

To sing a New Song – which is a Psalmodic and Apocalyptic invitation[6] – is to recognize the New Law: 'You have known the New Song: New Man, New Testament (and then) New Song.'[7] 'The New Song is the hymn of Grace, is the song of the New Man,'[8] who lives in the New Law of Love realized by Grace, and who sings while he works in conformity with the ten commandments: 'With these I will sing to you, with these I will give joy to you, with these I will sing a New Song, because the fullness of the law is love.'[9] But it is not enough to sing, one must sing well: 'Sing to him a New Song, sing well to him.'[10] Man must sing well because God wants to take pleasure in this song of man: 'He does not want it that his ears might be offended.'[11] Augustine talks of musical execution in order to describe the song sang well to God. That is to say, if someone were asked to sing well before an expert on music, he is apprehensive, and he knows that 'that which in you the non-expert would not notice, the expert [the artist] will reprove'.[12] For all of this, we should then sing to God to give him pleasure, understanding that he is – in this example – the Expert Artist par excellence.

The dimension of omnipresent pleasure in the musical thought of Augustine remains central also when he speaks of God. Just as in the way that the sense of hearing can become offensive or contrary to delight,[13] so too does God not care that his ears might be abused. The immutable which is not changed by the affect of music nonetheless wants to delight itself in the songs of men. God calls for a song fitting to his great love for man: he has given the New Song for love; he demands a song that is full of love. Therefore, the song, always moved by love, is assimilated to all songs because *song* is synonymous with *happiness*,[14] and love is not love without joy.

'Breathe in all our love, and sing the New Song. You sing it therefore not with your lips, but with your life.'[15] The feeling of the New Life – the feeling of being converted to a love that renovates man every time that he clothes himself in it – translates itself as to *sing well*. This musical paradigm includes then the transformation of the New Man, the affection of love and the expression of the New Law. The song therefore transcends its sonorous experience in order to express contemporaneously with its sound the New Law – love as the one way and the first commandment – plus the union of soul and body. The musical metaphor not only encloses the components of man in his various dimensions, but speaks of the end of this New Man perfected in love. The song always unifies the spiritual and material dimensions because they are allied – as are the thought of the heart with the actions of the body, and the rationality of words with the physics of sound, and then finally rationality itself with Rhythm itself.

To know the way in which one should sing to God is to know what will be pleasing to the Divine ears who 'know how to judge the singer', and who examine everything and who hear everything.[16] At this point, Augustine cannot help but make this a general question of musical theory. Namely, how could man hope, in theory even, to invent a song pleasing to the perfect ear? The answer is that he could not. Man could never hope to transform sonorous material into a musical form capable of pleasing the divine ears. God has made the human ear and hears all that is of man – 'Does he who implanted the ear not hear?'[17] – which means that to attempt to find a song that would satisfy becomes now impossible without his, God's, help. To accommodate this, man's weakness, the song of God Himself gets presented to man as a model to follow. Thus can the Artificer be seen to be shaping everything – even the fitting song that man returns to him. Verse 3 of Psalm 39 gives a clear rendering of how this New Song is actually placed upon man's lips by God: just as God had commanded the song of the sons of Moses, ordaining Moses to place it in their mouths, so he has done it of every man: the Song of the Lamb, sung upon the last day together with the Song of Moses.[18] The Divine Act clutches man from the abyss, it puts him in a stable place, there where he can receive the hymn of the Lord.

'See how He has even intoned the song for you, so that you hardly have to seek for its words. It is more that you just need to give form to this song which is already pleasing to the Lord. Sing it in joy!'[19] God rejoices in the joy of man. This is a recurring theme of the *Confessiones* and of *Enarrationes in Psalmos*. The Voice of God makes itself heard so that the voice of man might be possible. The Divine Word invokes the word of man which invokes the Divine Word in turn! The Song of God underlines the impossibility for man of finding within himself the words and form of the song that is pleasing to God. The second that he has received it from God (in the manner we have surveyed and specified), he intones it back to God and the song is by that means dissolved and resolved into pure sound. It is gone forever for what it was. We say that one does not sing joy, but *in joy*.

> [*Editor:* That is, one does not sing because one has received some intellectual listing on joy, which one afterwards retains.]

Thus, Augustine gives a definition of joy – or jubilation – that runs together song and the ineffable.

'What does jubilation mean? Simply to have heard without having had it explained in words that which with the heart you sing.'[20] When one sings in the heart, it is not necessary that one forms up words on the lips:

> Whosoever speaks expresses exteriorly, by means of articulated sound, a sign of his true will [in the matter], but God must be sought for and prayed for in the secret of the rational soul; which is of itself the definition of man.[21]

The articulated voice enunciates the thought or manifests the heart of the other, but God does not have need of exterior signs. When joy outruns reason, rational discourse must be silent. There is a form of joy of which words cannot speak, not even the beautiful song. This extreme happiness can only express itself in sound.

In fact, those who sing, both while they sow and while they reap, or while they are occupied with ardour in some other activity, may begin to sing in words expressing joy, however, when once a point is reached when they are so pervaded by happiness as to no longer be able to express themselves in words, they leave them behind those syllables of the words, and they abandon themselves to the sound of joy.[22]

An idea similar to this is expressed in the following passage from Psalm 99, in which we see in play this value and significance of *pure musical sound*.

He who jubilates does not pronounce words but emits sounds indicating happiness, without words. Jubilation is the voice of a heart inundated by joy, of a heart that, as far as it can, wants to manifest its affection, though without wanting to comprehend the significance of it. The man who is prey to joy puts it into exaltation, and from words that would not suffice for saying it or for comprehending it, he passes to cries of exaltation in which there are no words. From the sounds emitted, one sees very well that he is content but also that, made over in joy, he does not succeed in speaking the words of that which pleases him. We observe all of this in singers, also in the case of dishonest songs. Not that our jubilation should be like theirs! (We must jubilate in justice, they must jubilate in iniquity; we in confession, they in confusion.) However, to make you better to understand that which I am trying to show to you, I want you to turn in your minds instead to that which you already know; in other words, to what you have already seen of jubilation exemplified, in this case, in the workers of the fields. They, when they are satisfied with the abundance of a harvest, the sowers, and the reapers, or any other gatherer of fruit, sing and exalt, happy with the fertility and with the fecundity of the earth. Into such songs, expressed in words, are inserted also inarticulate cries that reveal the thrill of their souls in prey to Joy. And it is this that we call Jubilation.[23]

The affections, arising from the heart, are translated into musical sound. Augustine uses the image of the song of the farmers. This song is rehearsed by those closest to nature, as Augustine will also note in his *De Trinitate*, when he is describing the naturalness of the

Octave.[24] The song of the gatherers in the fields betrays a song most natural to man, that comes to him whether he is educated in music or not. A song of the earth no longer suffering, but exultant. A song of fecundity and of fertility with the body and soul participating in the abundance. And the abundance is abandoned in turn to joy, which crosses over the limits of reason and of song in order to concede everything to the *Pure Sound* – the inarticulate cry, the cry of exaltation.

If the voice is an articulated sound that conveys a signification,[25] the sound itself – qua sound – signifies the intention of the heart to make itself known – again, qua intention, that is, over and above (or under and beneath!) rational language. We are speaking of breath, sound, cry, silence: all *as they are*.

> The ineffable is in fact that which cannot be said: and if you cannot say it, but can yet feel it, what remains to you but to jubilate, and in a way in which the heart opens itself to a joy without words, a joy that dilates itself immeasurably big, to the point of bursting any syllables! Sing well to Him in jubilation.[26]

'Sing well to Him in jubilation' signifies to sing in an ineffable way, repeats Augustine in this second commentary on Psalm 32.[27] Joy expands itself beyond all meaning of words and to 'sing well' becomes the song that is filled with sound. This sound as the expression of the ineffability of happiness is linked up with the Augustinian theme of sound as the source of musical pleasure (*delectare*). As in, 'that which please you in song is a certain rhythmic measure of sound'.[28] To this rationality of sound in its rhythmic modulations, can be added or not the rationality of words. 'One can sing with the flute and with the chitara, and in such wise do the birds sing, producing a musical sound without words; as we do on these instruments when we make song, but not language.'[29] Augustine is saying that the pleasure of music does not depend on the significations of the words: 'when you sing, that which makes for the pleasure is not competence in language.'[30] Because the pleasure of music resides in sounds rather than words, the pure sound *is* the expression of pleasure and the *delectare* provoked by sound *is* the testament to joy, to praise and to jubilation.

If in the commentaries on Psalm 32 and Psalm 99, the sound of the voice is emancipated from words, in the commentary on

Psalm 46, jubilation is focused upon and inspires Augustine to reflect upon instrumental sound. The musical explanation is guided by the biblical text: 'God has ascended amid shouts of joy, the Lord amid the sounding of trumpets.'[31] The jubilation accompanies the Ascension of the Lord and is manifested through the sound of the trumpet.

Jubilation comes once again to be defined in relation to the ineffable: of certain joys, it is not possible to speak. These must be contemplated, meditated upon, conserved in the intimate places of the memory. It could happen to anyone. And it certainly happened to the Disciples when they witnessed Christ ascending into the Heavens.

> They wondered at it, full of joy; since this was a joy for which words could not serve, they did not hesitate to express in jubilation that which none could have explained. Therein was the sound of the trumpets, and the voice of the angels.[32]

The disciples expressed what they admired but could not compass round. And this very moment they sealed then in musical sound: the sound of the trumpet – instrument of warning and power par excellence[33] – and the voice of the angels.

After the Ascension, Christ removed himself from sight, but not from the heart, the place where he speaks and where resides his Song. Therefore, the Psalm continues, 'Sing praises to God, sing praises.'[34] Music returns even if the joy cannot be sung or recounted (before others). And so the characteristic of the hymn comes clear. As the mirror to the presence of the Absentee (Christ) in the heart, the hymn must proceed from the heart, must leave from it and then return to it afterwards.[35] When one searches for the right hymn, one must not search by the 'sound of the ear', but by the light of the heart.[36] In the Augustinian imagination, to find the fitting sound is to see by the light of the heart, wherein is generated an intelligible song that does not have need of resounding sensibly. The sound of the light of the heart is preferable to sensible sound because it cannot but be wise, in the way that sounded-out songs and hymns cannot.

If the mouth speaks, it may not match its owner's interior thoughts. It may be mere sounded material (in comparison). From this point of departure, Augustine develops the following analogy. Before Christianity, people adored and worshipped the constructions of their hands in idols, not understanding what they sang to these stones. One way to see this, would be to say that their hollow, unintelligent, automatic singing matched their stone gods! If these people, 'might have had an intelligent song, they would [surely] not have adored stones'.[37] The Christian does not see his God before him (in the manner of an idol), and so in that sense he does not obtain immediate, visible satisfaction that God has heard his song. His song therefore testifies to his faith first and foremost. Those who worship stones exhibit an easy, thoughtless faith, with the recipient of their song straight before them. The Christian is on an altogether different mission when he sings. His God is invisible to him and to others. Yet still he sings – and when he is giving his utmost, he sings silently, in his heart.

We have reached a concept central to the thought of Augustine: the silent song of the heart and the existence of an ineffable music which is wise, intelligent and delicious. This music quite simply is the ultimate level of expression, when it comes to mysteries human and Divine. If the sound without words – and liberated from the limits of syllables – carries man up to being able to manifest the joys that dilate his heart, this silent music of which we are speaking now carries him up yet again to being able to express the ineffable, and it draws him near to it.

The silent song of the heart

> Not with the voice of the body, whose sonority results from the vibrations of the air, but with the voice of the heart, which is silence to men but a great cry to God![38]

Sound as the manifestation of the unspeakable and of joy overflowing shares its properties of expression with silence, the other language over and above verbal language. 'By entering your room, you enter into your heart.'[39] There, 'you reach a place where it is silent.'[40] In this silence, the silent voice of the heart raises itself. 'My heart has said to you: I searched for your Face, in secret, where only you listen.'[41] The intensity of the word – and of the prayer – does not depend upon the power of the sound but on the collected presence – the condition of any intimate word and above all of silence.[42] In order to manifest thoughts profound and dear, concealed in the heart, the convening of words will not do (because they pass on as they come in). And no one wants that their most dear thoughts pass away. What takes over then so as to secure the situation is a loquacity of heart and of spirit. Whosoever speaks in his spirit quite simply passes over all words – passes over even himself – and takes pure joy in the Divine.[43] This transformation begins while a man reflects upon that which lives in his heart; then sees the light of it;[44] then hears it in spirit.[45]

The song gives testimony of the moment of passage from the Old man to the New. It contains the memory (literally, the 'record'!) and the passage; as in the musical metaphor of the Passion: that moment of passage between death and life. The song of the New Man is the song of the interior man:[46] he who sees now in his interiority things as they are beyond the mere appearance of them, he who sees what the Divine has hidden inside terrestrial reality. By this interior vision, this man is freed from the chains of his passions – jealousy, anger, cholera. Because he sings a New Song.

The interior man is expressed in the song of the heart, the only word that cannot lie or deceive. Whenever we read expressions like 'song of the heart' or 'sing with your heart', we should remember the biblical stage-setting: there, it is laid down that 'to speak with the heart *is* to think'.[47] There is an intimate alliance between the affection and the thought that accompanies it. In fact, the heart should not be considered the place of irrational affections in opposition to the mind. No, thinking and reasoning take place within it, too; that is, it is a place where they may take place.[48] And in the biblical and also in the Augustinian scheme, it looks to be the preferred place. That is to say, it is the place we think of when we talk of conscience and intellect and memory: the faculties that reply upon looking and listening to God.[49] The heart is the vital organ that gives the impulse of life to the other organs and that serves also as the seat of the affections that then live and mature inside it. Therefore, the Song of the Heart is the manifestation most intimate and silent of self-conscious affection.

[*Editor:* Think here of the pejorative, 'Heartless', and of how it is used. It is quite difficult in words to do what Laurence is attempting here, which is to build up the substantive case for the heart. This is because words and explanation work against the effort of it. And this is because bare logic and ratiocination is a cold mechanical process, the mere turning of cogs. It is, in fact, heartless; and this becomes my point. *Heart* really is at the heart of what it means to be human, and what we recognise as human. For example, the animals, too, think. The unblinking crocodile surveying his prey, thinks. But we call him 'heartless', and rightly so. Heart is so essential to what it means to be human that it is difficult to isolate it for analysis. Extract it for closer inspection, and it dies in your hands – Along with the life it supported. This is surely the point.]

The *Song of the Heart* must be considered together with the recurring expression 'ear of the heart': true listening – intimate, always right – the true listening of the ear that hears the inaudible, and pronounces it in the heart in the *words of silence*. The Song of the Heart therefore expresses for Augustine a word 'squared'. Squared because it multiplies the warning of Ecclesiastes – 'Guard your steps when you go to the house of God. Go near to listen rather than to offer the sacrifice of fools, who do not know that they do wrong.'[50] – by Jesus' warning on the blinding of pride – 'Immediately Jesus knew in his spirit that this was what they were thinking in their hearts, and he said to them, "Why are you thinking these things?"'[51] The song and the heart are both affective and rational, the seat of truth and the seat of understanding. Not only does the song have as its end the elevation of the mind to things Divine, but it helps us to comprehend the Psalm, too. It helps to introduce us to its significance.[52] In his act of interpreting a Psalm, and especially if it is going slowly and is arduous, Augustine will bring to mind the role of the song in comprehending the Sacred Text: 'Therefore we continue to sing, to the end of arriving at a greater clarity.'[53] The song helps, because with the sacred words now attaching to musical sound, the heart is better and more directly spoken to, it seems; in what amounts to a single instant of emotion and intelligence. The song offers a greater 'space' for understanding, not least because of the tears which liquify and run the otherwise hard and resisting words, locked in place otherwise in apparently endless discursive explanations.

[*Editor:* This is where I really do want to step in, and strongly, because we have reached the blasphemous climax of Laurence's book – Although, only apparently blasphemous. But still, that is the correct and accurate word, as you shall see. Laurence's whole book is brought into being because we have the Bible, the Christian Scriptures, and because we have Augustine, arguably their great interpreter. The Christian Scriptures are divided into the Old and New Testaments, with the New pointing a moral at the expense of the Old. This moral takes the form of a Person, God-Incarnate; and it consists therefore in setting the Spirit over the Letter. This at once separates Christianity from all other religions with nominally equivalent wisdom literatures and wise men by placing it in opposition to the letter, the word and language. In fact, *by placing it in opposition even to Itself on the page!* This is the zenith that Christianity climbs to, the eye of the needle, and so on. And it is completely confounding of everything, before and since. In other religions and science before Christianity and after it, written truth, or written laws, are what they are because they can be pointed to on the page and obeyed for what they are. They do not change. They certainly don't 'melt' or 'liquify', in Laurence's favourite picture. Truth, or law that is one thing today and the same thing tomorrow, and the next day, is why the human race has always lusted after truth, and looked for it in traditional religion and lately in the new religion of Western Science. And yet here is Christianity, with its message that shames all of this by calling it 'the letter', and 'Pharisaic', and setting over it the impossible alternative of the 'interpreted word' – The word that is made and remade endlessly in the hearts of those who read it or hear it; and which is made and remade according to the particular and personal wants and capacities of those hearts. Nothing could be farther from life on earth than this. On earth, we live in cities, by the laws; and the laws are said to be fair and just because they apply equally and indiscriminately to all. And yet (and again), here is Christianity to shame all of this by branding it positively inhuman, and to do it in a way that can be truly compelling, because it truly enough draws attention to our hearts and our souls and our supernatural selves. On the one hand, there is something broken about human life on earth that makes it that we really do need to live by the unfeeling Law. Yet on the other hand, in our hopes and dreams we are living for so much more! (We are living so eschatologically!) This is where Music enters; in general, and then especially for Augustine, and for Laurence. Because Music does really work against itself, and intrigue against itself, like the Christian Scriptures do. And in order to do this, it recruits human beings and inspires them to the task; again, as the Christian Scriptures do. Because on their own, they are nothing. They are words on paper, obeying the laws of words on paper – Again, just as Music is nothing when it is scored, obeying its own laws. And yet Music is so very obviously not that, because once having recruited its human, and entered her heart, she, and it, go where they will. Likewise, then, Augustine, when he is sitting down with the Sacred Scriptures; and the more so as he is given his example and his head start in the Psalmist.]

The music of the Ineffable Creator

He tends his hearing to that internal Voice of God, listening to its intimate and rational song. In this way, from on high, something resounds in silence. Not to the ears, but to the mind ... a sound extraordinarily good and fine, quite incomparable and ineffable.[54]

To the human music of works – whether in obeying commandments or in tribulation – we can add now a Divine music for contemplation. To the human music of the chitara or the harp comes this Divine song that really does come from on high in order to resound in silence. The Song of the Heart is now united to the Song of God, experienced internally, in a two-voice counterpoint. God sings in the heart of man so that the heart of man might sing. The Music of God is heard by him who tends his interior ear. Then, next, the human mind abstracts itself from the external clamour and concentrates itself on this new interior sound. The concepts of the internal Voice of God, of the Divine Rational Song, of the Ineffable Sound that provokes a *delectare* so-utterly-unsayable-as-to-be-incomparable(!), launch Augustine's reflections on the *Music of the Father*.

Augustine imagines the music of a Christian God who is close to men – in fact a God who lives in the heart of man. That is, he imagines God not only in his human nature, as made into sound and transformed into the musical instruments, but also in his

Divine nature, that is, inaccessible, incomprehensible, unenterable, unsayable, ineffable, and yet, close by virtue of his song in men's hearts. Of this silent song, Augustine will attempt to define its 'sound'; hoping to achieve something that will adequately reflect the Divine nature.

'The sound of that festival caresses the ears'

> In the house of God there is a never-ending festival: for there it is not an occasion celebrated once, and then to pass away. The angelic choir makes an eternal festival: the presence of God's face, joy that never fails. This is a festival of such a kind, as neither to be opened by any dawn, nor terminated by any evening. From that everlasting perpetual festivity, a certain sweet and melodious strain strikes on the ears of the heart, provided only the world does not drown the sounds. As he walks in this tabernacle, and contemplates God's wonderful works for the redemption of the faithful, the sound of that festival caresses his ears, and bears the hart away to the water-brooks.[55]

In his commentary on verse 5 of Psalm 41, in which the soul journeys to the House of God in the midst of songs, Augustine contraposes the instrumentalists who play in front of the House in order to call men towards its festival with the sound that proceeds from the House. Not by chance do we see again here contraposed the organ (*organum*) and the other instruments (*organa*), and the distinction is drawn out for us in the difference between the 'passengers' – the instrumentalists who play in front of the House – and the eternal sound proceeding from the House, and its angelic choir. Here we see the music of the Church being given a celestial justification, insofar as it can be seen as the image of this angelic choir. The perpetual song of the angels – conferred on them by their perpetual vision of the Face of God – finds in this identification with Church music one of its earthly echoes: 'From that eternal and perpetual festival resounds an "I don't know what kind of song, but how sweet it is to the ears of the heart!"'[56]

Yes, in the commentary on Psalm 41, musical sound occupies yet again a central position. But we are no longer speaking of the action of a sound of a power capable – with Divine intervention –

of collapsing the walls of a city.[57] We are instead in the presence of a power of sound that is Divine, but silent. This musical sound no longer exhibits its Divinity through its performativity, but in how it transforms through its sheer sweetness of silence. The supreme sweetness is neither a voice, nor a word, nor a melody nor a discourse, nor a music. It is a silence that 'speaks'.

The Divine song possesses the force to convert, to attract the soul of man and to carry it to a place of repose. This is no longer a question of Church music or sacred liturgy, insofar as that can truly enough help to elevate the individual spirit and cohere the community of believers around a single voice. Augustine's original, and famous, mistrust of these things comes back here, and cannot be forgotten! But now, he has a new and spectacular outlet for it. He can use it to valorize the sweetness of another musical sound. A musical sound that reverses – so to speak – and goes inside us, to seduce the soul and to carry it beyond all worded-out exterior music.

Augustine investigates the attraction of this interior music – the musical voice of the heart and the musical Voice of God. Because the interior musical sound does attract man towards the heights – which is the same thing as to say that it attracts him into his (spiritual) interior – he must as far as possible make silent about him – or ignore – all external clatter. He must ignore materiality and chatter! In order to describe the action of the sound of the Voice of God that echoes interiorly, and its properties, Augustine goes back into analogies with the musical instruments. His commentary on Psalm 41 distinguishes the residence of God on earth – namely, the Church, the Tabernacle – from his secret residence, which is his 'stable' House in Heaven.[58] Man must walk in the Tabernacle to reach the House of God, as the Psalmist did, in wonder:

> [While the Psalmist] was looking at the parts of the Tabernacle, he was led to the House of God, following a certain sweetness, an interior and mysterious wish which it is difficult to place, as if from the House of God was resounding sweetly an organ. And so while he was walking in the Tabernacle, he heard this sound interiorly, and was guided by its sweetness, following that which he felt resounding, abstracting himself from every carnal noise and from the noise of his blood, and reached at last the House of God.[59]

The theologico-musical concepts favoured by Augustine are all here in this dense musical metaphor. Interior joy is never completely comprehensible. There is in it something that reason just cannot investigate. As the heart of man remains in part hidden from him, so the joy that holds it in the breast is a mystery to its own sweetness. From the House of God resounds the sweet and soave sound of an organ: and now everything can be *Interior*, and because interior, secure. Completely secure.

The unsayable sweetness of musical sound serves to guide man inwards: 'he heard this sound interiorly, and was guided by its sweetness, following that which he felt resounding'. The being listens in his intimacy, and hears resounding a Voice – or better, a sound, an inarticulate sign, that says the unsayable and instils certainty. He lets himself be guided by this *Sweet-Certainty*, by his own new wish for it which escapes all rational comprehension.

Augustine now adds to this new wish and to its unspeakable sweetness and certainty the quality of joy, and he does this in order to stress how much this sweet wish, this inner certainty, is to be the Guide to be followed: 'Guided by the joyfulness of the intimate and intelligible sound.'[60] The sweetness of that which proves itself in the ineffable part of man's intimacy now becomes a secure sign. The sign of God who speaks outwith of all reason to touch the ears of the heart.

In its daily setting, this Music of God is there but difficult to attain. 'We sometimes arrive at it.'[61] This sound of unspeakable sweetness offers itself in certain moments of grace, and one catches glimpse of it. One hears it in moments of joy when grace is sufficiently present to carry one beyond oneself. However, this also means that the Divine sound is oftentimes absorbed into waking, mundane thoughts.[62] Whoever can escape from these daily things can hear it, can touch the Divine Face in sound.

For a moment, a moment of grace, a moment of evanescent perception given freely in love, we see with the eye of our heart the immutable in its reflection in interior sound, sweet and joyful. Then, as always, begins the dialogue of man with his soul: 'Why are you downcast, O my soul?'[63] And his soul, 'almost responding to him in silence' weeps because it can neither hold back nor hold on to the sweetness of the intimate moment.[64] 'It was in the tears that I remembered it':[65] as he cries, man is taken into a moment of intimate harmony within his heart. The soul is rapt with sweetness, but the vision of it flees. And yet man will and must try again, all over again. Every time that he leaves himself to be guided by the Voice of God in his heart.

There, in his stupor unknown and unexpected, man proves to himself, and feels for himself, what is his *Sweet-Certainty*, his 'occult wish'.[66] Occult, because the link between the affections and music *is* occult; as described, for example, by Augustine in his *Confessiones*. If you have made the experience of it, you can only go so far in depicting it afterwards. This is an occult wish that is ultimately and absolutely private to its owner and that is ultimately and absolutely true and certain *because* it is free.

'Delightful, incomparable and ineffable': A way to conclude

The highest listening is the listening to silence, and music perfects this in an ineffable sound. And this in itself is the height reached for by Augustine in his commentaries on the Psalms. Music achieves its maximum expression in the sound – experienced interiorly – of 'something that resounds from on high'.[67] This 'something', this *je ne sais quoi*, this call to the occult wish in us, is, like that wish, indecipherable. Thus, we are left able to say that music becomes the paradigm of silence, rather than that silence becomes the condition of music, or of music-making. He who hears this silent music, hears a sound of incomparable beauty. He hears silence itself become music, and music itself become silence.

This music takes leave of the sensible dimension in order to enter into a superior dimension, that of the very sounds of our intimacy, where in silence does sing the internal voice of conscience and indeed of consciousness. Here, we are talking always, then, of *The Other*. Of a message produced in the turn towards the heart of another (in a sympathy exhausting words), or to God Himself. Human interiority is identified with the presence of God and Augustine uses musical categories to speak of both. Voice, song and sound are all recalled to this project.

The drawing sound from the *House of the Father* combines with the song to God to form a diptych. As Augustine will put it in his commentary on Psalm 42, whoever hears this song will want to quieten all sensible sounds so as to hear instead this single extraordinary (spiritual) sound, at once *delightful, incomparable and ineffable*.[68] In turn and eventually, this single sound will become melodic: the sure sign that one has entered into silence's true harmony – the kind of harmony that we have noted before as like the rhythmic beating of the heart, which ultimately is indistinguishable from the silence which encloses it.

When sheltered from all external noise, this silent music sounds clear and strong – the music of he who finds repose in his heart and the music of God who sings in his sanctuary there.[69] Here, the concept and reality of *The Secret* is of the utmost importance, be it of the chamber of the heart,[70] of the House of the Father[71] or of the 'mansion of music'.[72] The human heart becomes music's nuptial bed, a protective structure surrounding the place of listening, of the silent word, of Divine and human song.

Musical silence becomes the voice of what is spoken intimately within, while the ear of the heart that perceives this silent sound allies itself to the 'interior eye' that sees the invisible. The melodies enter directly and penetrate deep, without mediation, where they give echo of the ineffability that was already in us. Mind and heart are united in the intelligence of heart that understands and does not err. The heart, in this its wise listening, is caught up in a joy always unexpected and always unimagined. With no words possible, all it can give in response is a silent gesture; or, in silence, the song of its rapture. This is that same stupor that did render Philo of Alexandria speechless. This silent sound of a joy provoked by 'something' (from the *House of the Father*) – something indescribable that explodes human reasoning – is the proper response of man to the sweetness of the Divine Song and to the silent music played on the organ of the *House of the Father*.

By means of all of this ineffable music, God asks man to regather and – as it were – reunite himself in a harmonious and amorous embrace,[73] to make himself capable again of hearing the sound of the loving voice,[74] to give himself up to its rhythmic touch, the erotic opening to the infinite.[75] The joy of this wish forthcoming is unspeakable (almost unbearable), and thus it tells of that which in man of the Divine is concealed.

There is always something untranslatable in this ecstasy of the internal and external senses.[76] And yet, who is there who does not know (instinctively) what they are seeing in the harmonious movements of two bodies or the voluptuousness of musical sound, or to seek for the secret reasons behind them and the hidden law? Who is there who does not (automatically) yearn to express it, however they have experienced it?[77] Thus, we say that the experience of delight is certain, even if it remains in part untranslatable.

We must be clear, the voluptuousness of bodies in love or the pleasure of the listener moved to musical sound is significant, not because they are tracks that will lead on to the Divine Reason in the end – that is, insofar as rhythmic movement numerated in the image of the Divine order becomes, in its eroticism, the very synonym of harmony[78] – but because they are already (conterminously) and justly sharing their occult property with the Divine music that is speaking to the heart of man, and moving it in an indefinable delight. Beauty is intimate, and proven in the intimacy of relationship, in the embrace, in the listening to music, in the listening to the interior music that sweetly leads man back to himself. *Delectatio, dulcedo* and *voluptas* qualify both human and Divine music: *Pleasure, sweetness* and *voluptuousness* recur again and again in the Augustinian considerations on the matter.

In fact, Augustine uses the exact same lexicon to describe human music as he does to describe Divine music when it achieves its effect. In both cases, it is always that *je ne sais quoi* that he stretches for – that unspeakable pleasure, that voluptuousness or eroticism that is utterly secure and recognized at once for what it is, even if it cannot be put into words afterwards. That sweet and soave sound. Thus, the difference between human and Divine music is not found, for Augustine, in their actions or in their characteristics. For with both, it is that sweetness that attracts; it is that voluptuousness that entraps the listener to carry them up to a higher hearing. It is not a question, then, of this pleasure being profane or not, or approached in degrees. No, because it is music that we are talking about, we simply cannot say where the human ends and the Divine begins. The only working distinction that Augustine will proffer is between the human senses involved. For example, the corporeal sounds of music-making penetrate the external senses in order to carry man inside himself. They play on his sensitivity to *delight* in order to elevate him to the act of contemplation. In this way, they help him to understand better the mystery contained in the words (of the Psalm) and to immerse himself in what is being sung. From there, the spiritual sounds begin to walk themselves in silence through his internal senses. This new, now silent music made upon these spiritual sounds is seen (then) to depart from interiority in order to return there again (renewed). Man is led inside himself only to return there again in better possession of himself and in better proximity to God.

In the Augustinian imagination, God is seen to lead man by means of sweet and joyful sounds. And by this stage, we are no longer talking of the Word of the Creator, conserving, consoling and curing, but of *Pure Sound*. In the same way that human music melts itself in the pure sound of joy and liberates itself from the limitations of language, so does *God the Musician* seduce and guide with the musical sounds of silence. The sound (as it were) of the 'rational' and internal song of God (Himself), and the sound of the Divine organ. This causes us to notice that this sound and this silence share their expressive properties at a level that is over and above (conventional) rationality and discourse, as well as applying equally to whatever it is that is unsayable in music (whether human or Divine).

Simply put, music translates the mystery that draws and unites. And again, this holds for human as much as for Divine music. Human music expresses this mystery, and in expressing it, manifests that it abides in a location only partly accessible to us (yet accessible to us still, and so the mystery of it).[79] This mystery always seems to refer to an eternal law that is removed from us in the first instance. But that yet again, does also come near to us and even into us through music's gateway, and music's gateway to pure sound. Perhaps better to say, then, that the connection between music and the affections is not *referable*.[80] The very act of being affected and moved displaces comprehension and removes altogether the option to understand through capture and definition – to understand *this*, only because it is an example of *that*. In this way, music accounts for the mystery of any sensible voluptuousness truly felt as well as for the reasons for attraction and encounter.

Thus does another musical element emerge from Augustine's commentaries on the Psalms, namely, the affection of the singer (of the Psalms) seen in its new and full theological perspective. This observation says that if this singer is not animated by love, they will only be able to sing formally and exteriorly. They will only be able to 'carry' their musical instrument, not play it. Before God, they will be mute. Again, because the words of the Psalm should acquire significance as they are sung, because the music which carries this song should acquire a sense over and above *Form*, because the Song of the Heart should be achieved, love must be present from the beginning.

So it is that the *Musical Man* offers a response to the Father that is both sung and silent, and which by being both, fulfils the *Law of Love*. That is, every time that he sends up the song of his heart, he follows *Christ the Celestial Intoner*. He lets himself be guided by the *Voice-Sound-Silence* of God and unites himself with his Creator. He becomes in fact re-created in the image of his Creator at the same time as he hears the ineffable sound of his Creator in his ear. To this *Music of the Ineffable*, man's only true and just response is the bowed and silent music of his heart – the music of the interior man.

As writer, priest and philosopher/theologian, Augustine came to see in musical imagery a way and a means of speaking of man in all his parts – soul, spirit, body; reason, mind, intellect; heart, affection, love; sense, bodily experience, action – plus a way and a means of speaking of the actions of Christ on earth in terms of Christ's human nature. And then of all of this, in such a way as to draw us closer to the *Eternal*. The image of God as a musician who consigns his law by playing, who intones a song that man below might sing, who makes this song to be utterly sweet and ineffable, who makes it to proceed from his house, played upon his Divine organ, all of this provides us with a way of thinking metaphorically and analogically on the secret nature of *The Father*. Thanks to these images – thanks to these musical images – we can at least attain to an idea, even if blurry. In fact, analogy is the only way and means available to us.

For example, in analogy with the sweetness of music, we are made to understand the otherwise paradoxical value of suffering and of the 'actions played upon the cithara' (as we pass in consciousness through this mortal life). We are made to understand them in terms of the sweetness of God. Here, two mysteries are brought together and opened in a musical image. The mystery of human suffering is able to be seen as being pleasing to the ear of God who hears it in the (internal) comprehension of his *Wisdom*. While the mystery of God as hidden to us in an inaccessible light becomes, in turn, justified through the musical image which makes this hiddenness and this inaccessibility the very condition of its sweetness.

The high great value of musical images over others in this regard is the affinity and kinship of music with the message and mystery of Christianity, namely, the union of reason and affection, of thought and action, of idea and sound; the non-referable nature of affection (how it always flees from full rational transfixion); and the ineffability of music understood as a mirror of *The Ineffable* and of the ineffability of human affection.

Then there is how the sheer sweetness of musical sound does resonate with this message and mystery of Christianity. As we have seen, without love, there can be no true music, whether sounded or silent; and whosoever loves, sings, insofar as song is the mirror of the desire of love. More, when God 'became sound' (Christ, God Incarnate), he united the chitara and the harp, earth and heaven, the corporeal and the transcendent, the body and the Divine symbol contained therein; and sufferings into miracles. He transformed himself into a musical instrument and died on the wood of the timbral for the love of men. For this same love of men, the Father creates and re-creates, leading man with sweet musical sounds and inviting him incessantly to find harmony, or the silent peace that God looks for in all things. Men are attracted to God's house where there they perceive a festivity, whose joy is but an echo of the full festivity awaiting them in eternity. These actions of attraction and seduction on the part of the Father cannot but be interpreted musically. They are simply too ready an analogy of the attraction of music to the soul, and how it can transport rapt listeners outside themselves.

This brings us out, finally, on how the musical image participates therefore in a theory of language and of language's limits. In his writings, Augustine never ceases to investigate that which man cannot comprehend, that which flees from his comprehension, that which he wants to know but cannot. He shows a tireless eye for the mysteries of the human psyche and the human will and heart. Man's heart is a mystery even to himself, even to itself. Not even the spirit that is in him can comprehend it.[81] Even as intellectual reason is overcome by the reasoning of the heart, so this reasoning of the heart overcomes proper comprehension. The conscience, along with the song of the heart in its trinitarian reflection of the soul – will, memory, reason – finds expression in music. Thus, music is seen to enjoy a privileged relationship to research and writing on the human soul. To the heart that loves, responds the silent song of the same. To the *je ne sais quoi* hidden in the heart, responds a *je ne sais quoi* in the music; notwithstanding whether that music be spiritual or sensible. While to the body, to the pleasure of experience and to the sensible voluptuousness of musical sound, make echo the occult and interior voluptuousness of silent music. We say that whatever is beyond words, has then music in which to take place.

At this height, Divine music and human music cannot be translated into words. Neither can the experience of beauty nor the beauty of experience be so translated. The ineffable is inherent in Divine nature as much as in music, and therefore the same way inherent in the experience of the Divine as in the experience of music. The limits of verbal language become obvious when man must attempt to describe his intimate and ecstatic and aesthetic experiences – whether in an encounter with another (human being) or with God. If sensible and spiritual music expresses this unspeakable mystery of meeting and encounter with that which attracts us to it, then we are left to say only this: whatever we may be able to say of Music, we shall never be able to pin down its *essence* (and that its whole magic is in that!).

NOTES

Premiss

1. I first began to experiment with this method in three contributions, published in *Divus Thomas, Commentarium de Philosophia et Theologia* (Wuidar, Laurence, '*Confessioni* e speculazioni musicali: l'immagine sonora nell'opera agostiniana', *Divus Thomas, Commentarium de Philosophia et Theologia*, 112, 2, 2009, p. 133–63; Wuidar, Laurence, 2010 'Parola segreta e trasporto gioioso: la metafora musicale nel commento agostiniano al salmo 32 e nel *De venatione sapientiae* di Cusano', *Divus Thomas, Commentarium de Philosophia et Theologia*, 113, 3, 2010, p. 66–84; Wuidar, Laurence, 2011 'Oltre le parole: suono, silenzio, sguardo, gesto. Teorie agostiniane e bernardiane del linguaggio affettivo', *Divus Thomas, Commentarium de Philosophia et Theologia*, 114, 3, p. 114–32). I then pursued it in various articles covering the musical symbolism in Philo of Alexandria and Gregory of Nyssa, in medieval mysticism in general and then of course in Augustine again (2015/1 and 2015/2, 2016, 2017/1 and 2017/2). See also my forthcoming 'Secret song and visionary music in Hadewich d'Anvers'. And there is much, too, in my book, distributed by Brepols, *L'uomo musicale nell'antico cristianesimo. Storia di una metafora tra Oriente e Occidente*, Bruxelles: Roma, Institut Historique Belge de Rome, 2016.
2. *Confess.*, III, 11, 19.
3. See, amongst others, *New Oxford History of Music*, vol. 2, 'The Early Middle Ages to 1300', R. Crocker & D. Hiley (eds.) 1990: 82–3, 233; Dyer, Joseph, 'Augustin and the "Hymni ante oblationem". The Earliest Offertory Chants?' *Revue des études augustiniennes*, 27, 1981, p. 85–99; Paredi, Angelo, 'Le innovazioni musicali di Sant'Ambrogio nei commenti di Sant'Agostino', *Rivista internazionale di musica sacra*, 9, 1988, p. 211–14; Parodi, Massimo, 'Agostino. La musica, i numeri e la relazione', V. Minazzi e C. Ruini (ed.), *Atlante storico della musica nel Medioevo*, Milano, Jaca Book, 2011, p. 40–5. The bibliography on this subject provided in the new

edition of *New Grove* is limited to writings from the 1930s to the early 1980s (with many general references). The only exception being made for the articles by the author of the entry, J. W. McKinnon. Four of his more recent contributions on psalmody and grade in the fourth century are included.

4   In the 1950s, Crossley noted the extent to which *De musica* was unknown, both to the general public and to musicians (not to speak of musicologists), and attributed this to its dialogue-form, stuffed with theology of little interest (the exceptions being the doctoral theses of Amerio 1929, contemporary with that of Edelstein 1929 and then a little later, Hoffmann 1931; with all three being cited by Perl & Kriegsman 1955: 496). Given this, Crossley proposed a brief schematic summary and presented that of Knight 1949, which allows the English reader without Latin to compass the text with ease. The same was to happen with various national publications of the treatise in these years. For example, Vecchi, Giuseppe, 1951 'Praecepta artis musicae collecta ex libris sex Aurelii Augustini De musica', *Memorie della Reale Accademia delle scienze dell'istituto di Bologna*, Classe di scienze morali, Ser. 5, 1, 1950, Bologna, Accademia delle scienze dell'Istituto di Bologna, p. 91–153. A few years later, on the occasion of the anniversary of the saint, came four pages (that begin with the caveat that the treatise would be better appreciated by a philosopher of music than an historian of music): Perl and Kriegsman 1955: 496–500. Around the same time, came the more considered and developed contribution of Perl, Carl J., 1954 'Augustinus und die Musik', *Schweizer. Musikzrg.*, 94, p. 402–41. In Germany, on the other hand, came a contribution focused entirely on just the sixth book of *De musica*: Schere 1909. Today, in Italy, two translations of *De musica* predominate. That of Bettetini, published in 1997 and that of Catapano, published in 2006. It is interesting to note that Augustine is absent (notwithstanding some general and insubstantial references) from the recent *The Cambridge Companion to Medieval Music*, M. Everist (ed.), 2011. Recently, Mahrt 2018 has focused on some of the Augustinian notions in medieval music and Prada Dussán 2015 has looked into the Latin; for example, *vestigium* and *signum* in the context of music.

5   For example, Honorato 1988: 153–96; Jordan, William, 1990 'Augustine on Music', Meynell (ed.), *Grace, Politics and Desire : Essays on Augustine*, Calgary, Alberta, The University of Calgary, p. 123–35; Massin, Marianna, 2011 'La musique selon saint Augustin, une rédemption du sensible?' F. Malhomme et E. Villari (ed.), *Muisca corporis. Savoirs et arts du corps de l'Antiquité à l'âge umaniste et classique*, Turnhout, Brepols, p. 139–58; Marrou, Henri-Irénée, 1938

Saint Augustin et la fin de la culture antique, Paris, De Boccard: 170; Micunco, Giuseppe, 2007 *Canta chi ama. La musica e il canto in sant'Agostino*, Bari, Stilo Editrice; Rey Altuna, Luis, 1960 'San Agustín y la música', *Augustinus* 5, p. 191–206; Schneider, A., 1939 'Aurelius Augustinus und die Musik', *Benediktinische Monatsschrift*, 21, p. 210–12; Sierra, José, 1986 'Agustin, enamorado de la musica', *La Escuela Agustiniana*, 24, p. 131–6.

6   See, for example, the following contributions from historians of theology or from musicologists (but from a theological point of view): Brennan, Brian, 1988 'Augustine's "De musica"', *Vigiliae Christianae*, 42, p. 267–81; Carol 2011: 27–45; Dussàn, Maximiliano P., 2003 'Lectura de los diálogos "De ordine" y "De musica" de San Agustín, a partir de la idea de ascenso del hombre hacia Dios a través de la música', *Franciscanum*, 45, p. 65–153; Guanti, Giovanni, 1987 'La musica come metafora teologica in Agostino e in Kierkegaard', *Rivista di Estetica*, 27, p. 153–69; Le Boeuf, Patrick, 1987 'Un commentaire d'inspiration érigénienne du De musica de saint Augustin', *Recherches Augustiniennes*, 22, p. 243–316; Matteucci, Giuseppe, 1985 '"De musica" des Hl. Augustinus: Musik als Wissenschaft des Geistes', *Der Hl. Augustinus, Vater der europäisch-afrikanischen Zivilisation. 5. internationale Konferenz des Schiller-Instituts, 1.-3. November 1985 in Rom*, Wiesbaden, Dr. Böttiger Verlags, p. 170–4; Perl, Carl J., 1937 'Musik und Geist. Die mus. Schriften des hl. Augustinus', *Musica sacra*, 65, p. 97–100; Piqué-Collado, Jorge A., 2006 *Teología y música: Una contribución dialécto-trascendental sobre la sacramentalidad de la percepción estética del Misterio (Augustín, Balthasar, Sequeri; Victoria, Schönberg, Messiaen)*, Roma, Pontificia Università Gregoriana; Pizzani, Ubaldo, 1978 'Spunti escatologici nel De musica di S. Agostino', *Augustinianum*, 18, p. 209–18; Pizzani, Ubaldo, 1990 'Intentio ed escatologia nel sesto libro del De musica di S. Agostino', L. Alici (ed.), *Interiorità e Intenzionalità in S. Agostino. Atti del I° e II° Seminario Internazionale del Centro di Studi Agostiniani di Perugia*, Roma, Institutum Patrisitcum Augustinianum, p. 35–57; Schneider, A., 1939 'Aurelius Augustinus und die Musik', *Benediktinische Monatsschrift*, 21, p. 210–12; Vagaggini, Cipriano, 1964 'La teologia della lode secondo S. Agostino', *La preghiera nella Bibbia e nella tradizione patristica e monastica*, C. Vagaggini e G. Penco (ed.), Roma, Edizioni Paoline, p. 399–467; Verheul, Ambroise, 1983 'La spiritualité du chant liturgique chez saint Paul et saint Augustin', *Questions liturgiques*, 64, p. 165–78; Walhout, Donald, 1989 'Augustine on the Transcendent in Music', *Philosophy and Theology*, 3, p. 283–93; Wiskus, Jessica, 2016 'Rhythm and

Transformation through Memory. On Augustine's Confessions after De Musica', *The Journal of Speculative Philosophy*, 30, 3, p. 328–38; England, F., 2017 'Music, Theology and Space. Listening as a Way of Seeking God', *Acta Theologica*, 37, 1, p. 18–40; Harrison, Carol, 2015 'Getting Carried Away. Why did Augustine Sing?' *Augustinian Studies*, 46, 1, p. 1–22; Harrison, Carol, 2019 *On Music, Sense, Affect and Voice*, New York, Bloomsbury, Reading Augustine.

7   To take just one example from many, see the introduction to the collection of texts (featuring passages from *De musica*) published by Bettetini in 1992. For a reading of *De Musica* from her, see Bettetini, MariaS, 2001 'Musica tra cielo e terra: lettura del De musica di Agostino d'Ippona', Mauro Letterio, *La musica nel pensiero medievale*, Ravenna, Longo, p. 103–22. On (amongst other things) the philosophical-musical terminology of Augustine, see Bettetini 1994. On the concept of temporal beauty, see Juarez, Agustìn U., 1998 'San Augstín. Belleza, música e istoria. "Un admirable cántico"', *Augustinus*, 169, p. 107–28.

8   Dehnert, Edmund J., 1969 'Music as Liberal in Augustine and Boethius', *Arts libéraux et Philosophie au Moyen Age. Actes du Quatrième Congrés international de philosophie médiévale, Université de Montréal, Canada, 24 aôut - 2 septembre 1967*, Montréal, Institut d'Etudes Médiévales, p. 987–91; Frova, Carla, 1985 'La musica nell'insegnamento delle arti liberali : i trattati di S. Agostino e Boezio', *Benedictina*, 2, 32, p. 377–88; Le Boeuf, Patrick, 1986 'La tradition manuscrite du *De musica* de saint Augustin et son influence sur la pensée et l'esthétique médiévale', *Positions de thèses*, Paris, Ecole des Chartes, p. 107–15; Pizzani, Ubaldo, 1994 'La "musica disciplina" tra Agostino e Boezio', A. Privitera (ed.), *Paideia cristiana. Studi in onore di Mario Naldini*, Roma, Gruppo Editoriale Internazionela, p. 347–64; Pizzani, Ubaldo, 2003a 'Du rapport entre le *De musica* de S. Augustin et le *De institutione musica* de Boèce', A. Galonnier (ed.), *Boèce ou la chaîne des savoirs. Actes du colloque international de la fondation Singer-Polignac, Paris 8-12 juin 1999*, Louvain-la-Neuve, Paris, Editions de l'Institut supérieur de philosophie-Editions Peteers, p. 357–77.

9   Beierwaltes 1975:140–57; Canettieri 1998: 150*ff.*; Crocker, Richard L., 1958 'Musica Rhythmica and Musica Metrica in Antique and Medieval Theory', *Journal of Music Theory*, 2, p. 2–23; Corbin, Solange, 1983 *La musica cristiana dalla origini al gregoriano*, Milano, Jaca Book (the Italian translation of: *L'Eglise à la conquête de sa musique*, Paris, Gallimard, 1963); De Crozals, J., 1894 'Quelques théories de s. Augustin sur la métrique d'après son traité de la musique', *Ann. enseign. sup. Grenoble*, 4, p. 499–540;

Eichhorn, Andreas, 1996 'Augustinus und die Musik', *Musica*, 50, p. 318–23; Guanti, Giovanni, 1990 'Tempo musicale e tempo storico in Agostino e in Kierkegaard', *Revue Esthétique*, 30, p. 95–141; Horn, Christoph, 1994 'Augustins Philosophie der Zahlen', *Revue des études augustiniennes*, 40, p. 389–415; Koller, H., 1981 'Die Silbenquantitäten in Augustinus's Büchen De musica', *Museum Helveticum*, 38, p. 262–7; Nowak, Adolf, 1975 'Die *numeri judiciales* des Augustinus und ihre musik-theoritische Bedeutung', *Archiv für Musikforschung*, XXXII, 3, p. 196–207; Phillips, Nancy and Huglo, Michel, 1985 'Le "De musica" de saint Augustin et l'organisation de la durée musicale du IXe au XIIe siècles', *Recherches Augustiniennes*, 20, p. 117–31; Pizzani 2000: 51–3; Proietti, Pierluca, 1999 'Numero e musica nel medioevo: Da Agostino alla complessità del Quattrocento', L. Mauro (ed.), *La musica nel pensiero medievale*, Ravenna, Longo, p. 71–80; Schmitt, Arbogast, 1990 'Zahl und Schönheit in Augustine "De musica, VI"', *Würzburger Jahrbücher für die Altertumswiss*, 16, p. 221–37; Van Wymeersch 2002: 41–6.

10 J. Bovet 1962; Charru, Philippe, 2009 'Temps et musique dans la pensée d'Augustin', *Revue d'études augustiniennes et patristiques*, 55, p. 171–88; Court, Raymond, 1987 *Sagesse de l'art*, Paris, Méridiens Klincksieck, p. 45–59, 62–71; Costa, Daniela, 1989–1990 *Il pensiero di sant'Agostino sulla musica*, Tesi di laurea dell'Università degli Studi di Torino; Michel, Alain, 1990 'Sagesse et spiritualité dans la parole et dans la musique: de Cicéron à saint Augustin', M. von Albrecht and W. Schubert (eds.), *Musik und Dichtung: neue Forschungsbeiträge, Viktor Pöschl zum 80. Geburtstag gewidmet*, Frankfurt, Lang, p. 133–44; Michelet, Marcel, 1943 'De la musique au silence. Notes sur l'usage de la joie esthétique d'après Saint Augustin', *Revue des Etudes Latines*, 21–2, p. 30–2; Meyer-Baer, Kathi, 1953 'Psychologic and Ontologic Ideas in Augustine's De musica', *The Journal of Aesthetics and Art Criticism*, 11, p. 224–30. The summary by Forman 1988: 17–27, 'Augustine's Music: "Keys" to the Logos' remains focused on *De musica* and its brief references to *Confessiones* does not capture the musical key to the Logos presented therein. Hentschel, Frank, 1994 'Sinnlichkeit und Vernunft in Augustins "De musica"', *Wissenschaft und Weisheit*, 57, p. 189–200; Hentschel, Frank, 2002 *De musica: Bücher I und VI: Vom ästhetischen Urteil zur metaphysischen Erkenntnis*, Hamburg, Meiner, Philosophische Bibliothek, 539; Pickstock, Catherine, 1998 'Ascending Numbers: Augustine's "De musica" and the Western Tradition', L. O. Ayres and G. Jones (eds.), *Christian Origins.Theology, Rhetoric and Community*, London-New York, Routledge, p. 185–215; Pickstock, Catherine, 1999 'Music: Soul,

City and Cosmos after Augustine', J. Milbank, C. Pickstock and G. Ward (eds.), *Radical Orthodoxy: A New Theology*, London-New York, Routledge, p. 243–77; Stefani, Gino, 1969 *L' Etica musicale di S. Agostino*, Roma, Pontificia Università Lateranensis; Walhout, Donald, 1989 'Augustine on the Transcendent in Music', *Philosophy and Theology*, 3, p. 283–93; Kim Hye Young, 2019 'Melody, Rhythm, Time. Phenomenology of Music in Augustine, Brentano and Husserl', *Glimpse*, 18, p. 61–9.

11 Bettetini, Marias, 1999 'Al limiti della materia, tra neoplatonismo e cristianesimo. Per una lettura del "De musica" di Agostino d'Ippona', T. Fuhrer, M. Erler and K. Schlapbach (eds.), *Zur Rezeption der hellenistischen Philosophie in der Spätantike*, Franz Steiner Verlag, Stuttgart, p. 123–38; Gonzalés, Paloma O., 2005 *El De musica de san Agustín y la tradición pitagórico-platónica*, Valladolid, Estudio agustiniano; Pabón, Guillermo L.C., 2011 *Numerus-proportio en el De Musica de San Agustín: La tradición pitagórico-platónica*, Editorial Académica Española; Pugliatti, Salvatore, 1947 'S. Agostino e l'estetica musicale dei Greci', *Teoremi*, 2, p. 182–99; Sallmann, Klaus, 1990 "Augustinus' Rettung der Musik und die antike Mimesistheorie", H. Eisenberger (ed.), *Epmheymata. Festschrift für Hadwig Hörner zum sechzigsten Geburtstag*, Heidelberg, Carl Winter-Universitätsverlag, p. 81–92.

12 Bowen, William R., 1988 'St. Augustine in Medieval and Renaissance Musical Science', R. R. La Croix (ed.), *Augustine on Music. An Interdisciplinary Collection of Essays*, New York, Edwin Mellen Press, p. 29–51; Brown, Howard Mayer, 1984 'St. Augustine, Lady Music, and the Gittern in Fourteenth-Century Italy', *Musica Disciplina*, 38, p. 25–65; Corbin, Solange, 1962 '"Musica" spéculative et "cantus" pratique. Le rôle de saint Augustin dans la transmission des sciences musicales', *Cahiers de civilisation médiévale*, 5, p. 1–12; Föllmi, Beat, 1994 *Das Weiterwirken der Musikanschauung Augustins im 16. Jahrhundert*, Bern, Peter Lang (Europäische Hochschulschriften, XXXVI/116); Goldman, David, 1985 'Augustinus und die Möglichkeit einer musikalischen Renaissance', *Der Hl. Augustinus, Vater der europäisch-afrikanischen Zivilisation. 5. internationale Konferenz des Schiller-Instituts, 1.-3. November 1985 in Rom*, Wiesbaden, Dr. Böttiger Verlags, p. 175–88; Le Boeuf, Patrick, 1986 'La tradition manuscrite du *De musica* de saint Augustin et son influence sur la pensée et l'esthétique médiévale', *Positions de thèses*, Paris, Ecole des Chartes, p. 107–15; Panti, Cecilia, 2007 '*Verbum cordis e ministerium vocis*. Il canto emozionale di Agostino e le visioni sonore di Ildegarda di Bingen', in M. Cristiani, C. Panti and G. Perillo (eds.), *Armonia mundi*.

Musica Mondana e Musica Celeste fra Antichità e Medioevo, Firenze, Edizioni del Galluzzo, p. 155–87; Vendrix, Philippe, 1992 'L'Augustinisme musical en France au XVIIe siècle', *Revue de Musicologie*, 78, p. 237–55.

13 Cf., for example, Panti, Cecilia, 2010 'Il suono che tace. Silenzio e pausa in Sant'Agostino e nella teoria musicale medievale', *Micrologus*, 18, p. 3–28; Mahrt, William P., 2018 'St. Augustine's Time and Eternity in Medieval Music', *Sacred Music*, 145, 4, p. 6–14.

14 See Fubini, Enrico, 1976 *L'estetica musicale dall'antichità al Settecento*, Einaudi, Torino and Panti, Cecilia, 2008 *Filosofia della musica. Tarda Antichità e Medioevo*, Roma, Carocci.

15 'Tristesse de l'historien', *Esprit*, 1. 04. 1939.

16 As I have indicated, references to this can be found all across the literatures on medieval music. See in particular Lemos, Fernando A., 2001 '"Proportio habens medium duoque extrema". A média aritmética e média harmónica nas "Confissões", de Santo Agostinho', *Actas do congresso internacional, as Confissões de Santo Agostinho*, Lisboa, Universidade Católica Editora, p. 671–96; Morao, Artur, 2001 'A musica como realidade e como metafora, nas "Confissões"', *Actas do congresso internacional, as Confissões de Santo Agustinho*, Lisboa, Universidade Católica Editora, p. 729–44; Panti, Cecilia, 2010 'Il suono che tace. Silenzio e pausa in Sant'Agostino e nella teoria musicale medievale', *Micrologus*, 18, p. 3–28 (in the first part of this article, (pp. 6–17), the author adds to and deepens the hitherto known parallels between *De musica* VI and *Confessiones* XI); Pizzani, Ubaldo, 2003b 'S. Agostino e la musica alla luce delle "Confessioni"', *Le 'Confessioni di Agostino (402-2002). Bilancio e prospettive, XXXI Incontro di studiosi dell'antichità cristiana, Roma, 2-4 maggio 2002*, Roma, Institutum Patrisitcum Augustinianum, p. 487–98; von Albrecht, Micheal, 1993 'Zu Augustinus Musikverständnis in den "Confessiones"', G. W. Most (ed.), *Philanthropia kai Eusebeia. Festschrift für Albrecht Dihle zum 70. Geburtstag*, Göttingen, Vandenhoeck & Ruprecht, p. 1–16; Wiskus, Jessica, 2016 'Rhythm and Transformation through Memory. On Augustine's Confessions after De Musica', *The Journal of Speculative Philosophy*, 30, 3, p. 328–38; Boccadoro, Brenno, 2019 'Remarques sur les essais sur l'origine de la musique où il est parlé d'ornithonlogie', *Poésie*, 167–8, 1–2, p. 89–111.

17 For example, McKinnon, James W., 1968 'Musical Instruments in Medieval Psalm Commentaries and Psalters', *Journal of the American Musicological Society*, 21, p. 3–20; Skeris, R., 1984–1985 '*Via nova, viator novus, canticum novum*. The Theology of Praise in Song According to Augustine's *Discours on the Psalms*',

Musices aptatio, p. 69–100; Paredi, Angelo, 1988 'Le innovazioni musicali di Sant'Ambrogio nei commenti di Sant'Agostino', *Rivista internazionale di musica sacra*, 9, p. 211–14. In the field of theology, see Zorzi, Benedetta M., 2002a 'L'esperienza del canto liturgico secondo le *Enarrationes in Psalmos* di Sant'Agostino', *Inter Fratres*, 52, 1, p. 27–52; 52/2, p. 211–38.

18 Cf., for example, Gamber, Klaus, 1969 'Ordo Missae Africanae. Der nord-afr. Messritus zur Zeit des hl. Augustinus', *Röm. Quartalschrift für christl. Altertumskunde und Kirchengesch*, 64, p. 139–53.

19 Fedriga 1976–7: 5–17; Perl & Kriegsman 1955: 496–50. On jubilation, these authors cite the comments on Psalms 32, 94 and 56; Zorzi, Benedetta M., 2002b 'Melos e Iubilus nelle Enarrationes in Psalmos di Agostino. Una questione di mistica agostiniana', *Augustinianum*, 42, p. 383–413. On music number symbolism, see Fritz, Jean-Marie 2018 'Cithares à géométrie variable dans les exégèses médiévales des Psaumes ou Comment la pensée sérielle crée l'instrument de musique', in *La pensée sérielle, du Moyen Age aux Lumières*, Cahiers de recherche des Instituts néerlandais de langue et de littérature française, 65, Leiden, Brill, p. 108–28.

20 Gerold 1931. In this thesis, presented to the Protestant Faculty of Theology at Strasbourg, the author cites (with little elaboration of his own, but indexing many other passages in patristics) various of Augustine's comments that relate to music, but particularly, to jubilation and to allegories made upon musical instruments (on jubilation, the comments on Psalms 32 and 99, pp. 121–2; on allegories, the comments on Psalm 32, pp. 111–12, 128–30 and on Psalm 149, p. 131). For a deeper work on musical allegory in Augustine's commentaries on the Psalms, see Costa, Daniela 1993 'Sant'Agostino e le allegorie degli strumenti musicali', *Répertoire International d'Iconographie Musicale*, 28, p. 207–26; Zorzi, Benedetta M., 2007 'Cuori con-cordi ma non all'uni-sono. L'allegoria alla vita cristiana della *vox strumentalis* nelle *Enarrationes in Psalmos* di S. Agostino', *Reportata. Passato e presente della teologia* [rivista in linea], http://mondodomani.org/reportata/zorzi07.htm; Folli, Laura, 2001 '"Canticum cordis": la musica e l'interiorità nelle Enarrationes in Psalmos di Agostino', in Mauro Letterio, *La musica nel pensiero medievale*, Ravenna, Longo, p. 177–84; and from researchers in theology rather than in musicology, see Zorzi 2002a and Zorzi, Benedetta M., 2007 'Cuori con-cordi ma non all'uni-sono. L'allegoria alla vita cristiana della *vox strumentalis* nelle *Enarrationes in Psalmos* di S. Agostino', *Reportata. Passato e presente della teologia* [rivista in linea], http://mondodomani.org/reportata/zorzi07.htm; Grossi, Vittorino, 'L'immagine musicale nelle Enarrationes in Psalmos di Agostino: L'interazione con la teologia "affetttiva"', *Augustinianum* vol. 56, Issue 1, June 2016, 207–33; Folgeman 2019: 133–50.

Introduction

1 See, for example, Ludwig Wittgenstein, *Tractatus Logico-Philosophicus*, London, Routledge, 1977, 47: 'In a certain sense, we cannot make mistakes in logic. Self-evidence, which Russell talked about so much, can become dispensable in logic, only because language itself prevents every logical mistake. – What makes logic a priori is the *impossibility* of illogical thought.'
2 Cf. *De mus.*, VI, 11, 32; *De Trin.*, VII, 6, 9.
3 Cf., for example, *Conf.*, X, 33, 49; *De Trin.*, XII, 14, 23.
4 Cf., *De Trin.*, XII, 14, 23: 'Or if one were to apprehend the rhythm of any artificial or musical sound, passing through certain intervals of time, as it rested without time in some secret and deep silence, it could at least be thought as long as that song could be heard; yet what the glance of the mind, transient though it was, caught from thence, and, absorbing as it were into a belly, so laid up in the memory, over this it will be able to ruminate in some measure by recollection, and to transfer what it has thus learned into systematic knowledge.'
5 Cf., for example, *Conf.*, XII, 31, 41.
6 Cf. *De vera rel.*, 50, 98.
7 See 1 Cor 13, 12.
8 Cf., Arthur Schopenhauer's thoughts on the matter, from his *Die Welt als Wille und Vorstellung*, quoted here in Harlow Gale, 'Schopenhauer's Metaphysics of Music', *New Englander and Yale Review* vol. 48, no. CCXVIII (1888), p. 362: 'Music does not express this or that particular and definite joy, this or that sorrow, or pain, or horror, or delight, or merriment, or peace of mind; but joy, sorrow, pain, horror, delight, merriment, peace of mind themselves, to a certain extent in the abstract, their essential nature, without accessories, and therefore without their motives. Yet we completely understand them in this extracted quintessence. Hence it arises that our imagination is so easily excited by music, and now seeks to give form to that invisible yet actively moved spirit world which speaks to us directly, and to clothe it with flesh and blood, that is, to embody it in an analogous example. This is the origin of the song with words, and finally of the opera, the text of which should therefore never forsake that subordinate position in order to make itself the chief thing and the music the mere means of expressing it, which is a great misconception and a piece of utter perversity; for music always expresses only the quintessence of life and its events, and never these themselves, and therefore their differences do not always affect it. It is precisely this universality, which belongs exclusively to it, together with the greatest determinateness, that

gives music the high worth which it has as the panacea for all our woes. Thus if music is too closely united to words, and tries to form itself according to the events, it is striving to speak a language which is not its own.'

9 Cf., *Conf.*, VIII, 12, 29.
10 Cf., *Conf.*, XII, 29, 40.
11 [*Editor:* This is the difference between Platonic idealism and the Augustinian Christian supernaturalism. It is the difference between (on the example and subject of this book) the purely mental thrill of realizing that music cannot escape from the numbers which afterwards describe it and the purely supernatural thrill of realizing that that is exactly what it has done, if it has moved you. As Augustine is so often at pains to show, Platonism, but most superbly Plato's tale of the formation of the world in his *Timaeus*, is as true a rendition of Christian fact on the matter (Monotheism) as one is likely to hope for. So true, in fact, that he surmises that Plato, on his famous visit to Egypt, might well have taken a chance to study the Hebrew Scriptures then being kept in that land and in the process of being translated into Greek on the orders of King Ptolemy (See *De civ. Dei*, VIII, 12). HOWEVER, these word-formulations which correctly describe what exists and correctly attribute it to the one true God, come to nothing if they are as far as one goes. Hence Augustine's oft-repeated warning to Christian wisemen, after the Apostle, to 'be wary of those who practice philosophy "according to the elements of the world" (Coloss. 2.8) and not according to God, by whom the world itself was made' (*De civ. Dei*, VIII, 10). These 'elements of the world', of which the numbers in music are a prime example, are always there to be seen, and true philosophy truly sees them. But this endless documenting of reality becomes ironic after a while, and very definitely prideful and harmful, if it is practiced for its own sake. What music instead can show, when taken seriously; and what God shows when he speaks and what we show when we respond to his ineffability with the ineffability in us; is that the description and documentation of what is there in the universe to be described and documented à la Platonism or Science is a tautology (hence Augustine's accusation of 'irony' and 'pride'), which only becomes what it truly should become (under the Augustinian Christian God) when that same tautology and its naturalism is set against supernaturalism (rather than yet another naturalism, to simply enlarge and extend that same tautology). This was something for which Augustine really did have the master's eye. Plus, he pursued it relentlessly. Plus, he systematically overcame by means of it, the gamut of highfalutin and commonplace scientific objections to

the Christian God and the Christian Scriptures. Thus, to Augustine – to the mature Augustine – we have the physical spectacle of music and mathematics or the physical spectacle of speech and language ONLY to supply the rational definitions of the same which we then posit of God, and / or of ourselves when we are being, or being receptive to the soulful and the supernatural. Augustine takes the soulful and the supernatural seriously, and begins with it always. Thus, God is said to 'speak', or 'sing', or 'play' not on condition of the single, technical definitions of those acts supplied by the laws of nature and which humankind is obliged to follow in the Earthly City, but on 'condition' (if that is now the word) of their original, ineffable taking place in the Heavenly City and in God's abiding eternity. See, for example, *De civ. Dei*, XVI, 6: 'But God does not speak to the angels in the way that we speak to each other, or to God, or to the angels, or as the angels speak to us, or as God speaks to us through them. Rather, he speaks in his own ineffable way. His speech is explained to us in our fashion; but God's speech is indeed more sublime than ours. It precedes his action as the immutable reason of the action itself, and it has no audible and transient sound, but it has a power which endures for eternity and operates in time. It is in this way that he speaks to the holy angels, whereas he speaks to us, who are situated far away from him, in a different way. And yet, when we also grasp something of this kind of speech with our inward ears, we ourselves come close to the angels. There is no need in this work, then, for me to give repeated explanations of God's "speaking". For the immutable Truth either speaks by itself, ineffably, to the minds of rational creatures, or it speaks through a mutable creature: either to our spirit by spiritual images, or to our corporeal sense by corporeal voices.']

12 See *De mus.*, I, 4, 6.
13 See *De ord.*, I, 8, 25.
14 See *De vera rel.*, 41, 77.
15 See *De vera rel.*, 42, 79.
16 See *De vera rel.*, 22, 42; *De mus.*, VI, 8, 21; *Imm. an.*, 3, 3.
17 See, for example, *Conf.*, XI, 22, 18.
18 See *De mus.*, VI, 11, 33.
19 See his *Sermones super Cantica Canticorum*, LXVII.
20 From *Ep.*, 118, worth quoting from at length for those unaccustomed to the debates of the time and their turning points: 'As you are aware, all questions in the pursuit of wisdom are classified under three heads – Ethics, Physics, and Dialectics. When, therefore, the Epicureans said that the senses are never deceived, and, though the Stoics admitted that they sometimes are mistaken,

both placed in the senses the standard by which truth is to be comprehended, who would listen to the Platonists when both of these sects opposed them? Who would look upon them as entitled to be esteemed men at all, and much less wise men, if, without hesitation or qualification, they affirmed not only that there is something which cannot be discerned by touch, or smell, or taste, or hearing, or sight, and which cannot be conceived of by any image borrowed from the things with which the senses acquaint us, but that this alone truly exists, and is alone capable of being perceived, because it is alone unchangeable and eternal, but is perceived only by reason, the faculty whereby alone truth, in so far as it can be discovered by us, is found? Seeing, therefore, that the Platonists held opinions which they could not impart to men enthralled by the flesh; seeing also that they were not of such authority among the common people as to persuade them to accept what they ought to believe until the mind should be trained to that condition in which these things can be understood – they chose to hide their own opinions, and to content themselves with arguing against those who, although they affirmed that the discovery of truth is made through the senses of the body, boasted that they had found the truth. And truly, what occasion have we to inquire as to the nature of their teaching? We know that it was not divine, nor invested with any divine authority. But this one fact merits our attention, that whereas Plato is in many ways most clearly proved by Cicero to have placed both the supreme good and the causes of things, and the certainty of the processes of reason, in Wisdom, not human, but divine, whence in some way the light of human wisdom is derived – in Wisdom which is wholly immutable, and in Truth always consistent with itself; and whereas we also learn from Cicero that the followers of Plato laboured to overthrow the philosophers known as Epicureans and Stoics, who placed the supreme good, the causes of things, and the certainty of the processes of reason, in the nature either of body or of mind – the controversy had continued rolling on with successive centuries, so that even at the commencement of the Christian era, when the faith of things invisible and eternal was with saving power preached by means of visible miracles to men, who could neither see nor imagine anything beyond things material, these same Epicureans and Stoics are found in the Acts of the Apostles to have opposed themselves to the blessed Apostle Paul, who was beginning to scatter the seeds of that faith among the Gentiles.'

21 *Ep.*, 159.
22 See, for example, *De ord.*, II, 11.

23 Cf., *En.*, 89, 10; 150, 1.
24 *En.*, 6, 2.
25 Cf., for example, *Serm.*, 9, 6–7.
26 *En.*, 47, 1.
27 See *En.*, 12, 6.
28 See *En.*, 47, 8.
29 *En.*, 39, 6.
30 *En.*, 39, 6.
31 For a definite statement of its necessity, both for understanding the words of another and for understanding any thing, see: *Conf.*, X, 1, 3.
32 *En.*, 30 II disc. 3, 1.
33 Cf. *En.*, 38, 1.
34 Pier Paolo Pasolini, 'Lettera da Benares', in Pier Paolo Pasolini, *L'odore dell'India* (Milano, Garzanti, 2016), p. 123.

Chapter 1

1 See Gen 1, 26–7.
2 *En.*, 92, 1.
3 *En.*, 48 disc. 2, 11.
4 See Gen 1, 3–26; Ps. 148, 5.
5 See Gen 1, 26.
6 *En.*, 49, 3.
7 See *De civ. Dei*, X, 19.
8 See *En.*, 44, 7 and 9.
9 Cf., for example, *En.*, 39, 13.
10 *En.*, 39, 4.
11 *En.*, 39, 4.
12 See *En.*, 38, 4.
13 *En.*, 55, 7.
14 Mt 13, 9.
15 Cf., *En.*, 25 II, 11.
16 *En.*, 25 II, 11.
17 Ps. 31, 9.
18 For these last number of quotes, see *En.*, 71, 1: 'Hymns are praises of God accompanied with singing: hymns are songs containing the praise of God. If there be praise, and it be not of God, it is no hymn: if there be praise, and God's praise, and it be not sung, it is no hymn. It must needs then, if it be a hymn, have these three things, both praise, and that of God, and singing. What is then, there have

failed the hymns? There have failed the praises which are sung unto God. He seems to tell of a thing painful, and so to speak deplorable. For he that sings praise, not only praises, but only praises with gladness: he that sings praise, not only sings, but also loves him of whom he sings. In praise, there is the speaking forth of one confessing; in singing, the affection of one loving (*in cantico amantis affectio*).'

19 See *En.*, 76, 4.
20 *Serm.*, 34, 1: 'Canticum res est hilaritatus, et si diligentius consideremus, res est amoris. Qui ergo novit novam vitam amare, novit canticum novum cantare.'
21 *Serm.*, 34, 6.
22 *En.*, 76, 4.
23 *Serm.*, 34, 4.
24 *Serm.*, 34, 6.
25 See Thomas Aquinas, *Summa Theologiae*, II, II, 180, 1.
26 *En.*, 72, 4.
27 Cf. *En.*, 72, 6.
28 Cf. *En.*, 72, 3.
29 Cf. *En.*, 49, 21.
30 Ps. 55, 12; *En.*, 49, 21.
31 *En.*, 49, 21.
32 Cf. *En.*, 53, 8.
33 *En.*, 53, 10.
34 Cf. *En.*, 53, 10.
35 Ps 48, 5; *En.*, 48 I, 5.
36 See *En.*, 48 I, 2.
37 Matt. 13, 9.
38 See *En.*, 48 I, 5.
39 *Conf.*, VIII, 10, 16; ' ... auditor in corde ... '
40 *En.*, 48 I, 5.
41 Nicholas of Cusa, *De venatione sapentiae*, 5, 20.
42 This idea one finds put forth repeatedly by Augustine. For example, in his commentary on verse 7 of Psalm 49: 'listen, and I will speak to you – if you listen, there will be no silence ... if you do not listen, even while I am speaking, I will not be speaking to *you*' (*En.*, 49, 14). Likewise, in his commentary on verse 13 of Psalm 50.
43 *En.*, 50, 13.
44 *En.*, 48 I, 5.
45 *En.*, 48 I, 5.
46 Matt. 13, 9.
47 See 1 Cor 13, 12.
48 *En.*, 48 I, 5: 'Aenigma est obscura parabola quae difficile intellegitur. Quantumvis excolat homo cor suum, et ad interiora intellegenda

refugiat, quamdiu per corruptibilitatem carnis huius videmus, ex parte videmus.'
49 *Ep.*, 138, 1, 5.
50 *En.*, 39, 9.
51 *En.*, 26 II, 12.
52 *En.*, 26 II, 12.
53 *En.*, 26, II, 12.
54 *En.*, 26 II, 12.
55 *De mus.*, I, 2.
56 *De mus.*, VI, 11, 31.
57 *En.*, 26 II, 12.
58 Pseudo-Dionysius the Areopagite, *I nomi divini*, I, 1, 4, 588A, in *Dionigi Areopagita, Tutte le opere* (eds. Piero Scazzoso and Enzo Bellini) (Milano, Bompiani, 2009), p. 361.
59 *En.*, 26 II, 12.
60 *En.*, 35, 14.
61 *En.*, 35, 14.
62 *En.*, 35, 14.
63 *En.*, 36 II, 8.
64 Ps. 26, 7; *En.*, 26 II, 14.
65 *En.*, 12, 6.
66 Cf. *En.*, 17, 50: '"And I will praise your name": None better shall you see it, than in my good works.'
67 Cf. Origen, *Tractatus in Psalmos*, 91, 4.
68 See *En.*, 32 II disc. 1, 4–8.
69 See *De civ. Dei*, X, 12.
70 *En.*, 42, 5.
71 *En.*, 80, 5.
72 *En.*, 42, 5.
73 Job 1, 21; *En.*, 32 II disc. 1, 5: 'cithariza securus; certus in Deo tuo, tange chordas in corde, et dic tamquam in cithara in inferiore parte bene sonante: Dominus dedit, Dominus abstulit; sicut Domino placuit, ita factum est: sit nomen Domini benedictum.'
74 *En.*, 32 II disc. 1, 5.
75 *En.*, 32 II disc. 1, 5.
76 *En.*, 32 II disc. 1, 5.
77 Ps. 42, 5.
78 *En.*, 42, 5.
79 *En.*, 42, 5.
80 *En.*, 42, 5.
81 *Contra Prisc. et Orig.*, VIII, 11.
82 See *En.*, 32 II disc. 2, 10. Augustine is here referring to the traditional method of trumpet manufacture.

83 *En.*, 42, 5; Ps. 42, 4.
84 See Rom 5, 34; *En.*, 42, 5.
85 *En.*, 42, 5.
86 *En.*, 42, 5.
87 Ps. 42, 5.
88 Ps. 42, 5; *En.*, 42, 6.
89 Matt. 26, 38.
90 Cf. *En.*, 89, 7.
91 See *De mus.*, VI, 4.
92 *De mus.*, VI, 5, 14.
93 *De mus.*, VI, 5, 14.
94 Cf. *De mus.*, VI, 5, 11.
95 *De mus.*, VI, 5, 9.
96 *De mus.*, VI, 5, 12.
97 *De mus.*, VI, 5, 12.
98 Cf. *De mus.*, VI, 5, 12.
99 *De mus.*, VI, 8, 21.
100 Bonaventura, *Vitis mystica*, VII–XIII.
101 See Matt. 27, 46.
102 *En.*, 32 II, disc. 1, 6.
103 *En.*, 32 II disc. 1, 6.
104 *En.*, 32 II disc. 1, 6.
105 *En.*, 32 II disc. 1, 6.
106 *En.*, 32 II disc. 1, 6.
107 Gal. 5, 14.
108 1 Cor 13, 1.
109 *En.*, 80, 5.
110 Ps. 80, 3; *En.*, 80, 5.
111 *En.*, 80, 4.
112 *En.*, 80, 4.
113 See *En.*, 91, 3 & 4.
114 Ps. 92, 2–4.
115 See *En.*, 91, 3.
116 *En.*, 91, 3.
117 *En.*, 91, 4.
118 *En.*, 143, 16: 'Caeterum qui non habent caritatem, portare psalterium possunt, cantare non possunt.'
119 *En.*, 91, 4.
120 *En.*, 91, 5.
121 *En.*, 91, 5.
122 *En.*, 42, 8.
123 *En.*, 42, 7.

Chapter 2

1. *En.*, 19, 1.
2. *En.*, 109, 7.
3. *En.*, 109, 7.
4. 1 Sam 16, 23.
5. 2 Kings 3, 15.
6. See *En.*, 26 II, 1: 'Ita utrumque verum est, et nostrum esse vocem, et nostram non esse; et Spiritus Dei esse vocem, et ipsius non esse.'
7. *En.*, 50, 11.
8. Philo of Alexandria (eds. Giovanni Reale and Roberto Radice), *L'erede delle cose divine* (Milano, Rusconi Libri, 1994).
9. See his *De natura corporis et animae*, 65–70.
10. *L'erede delle cose divine*, 3.
11. *L'erede delle cose divine*, 4.
12. Dt 27, 9.
13. *L'erede delle cose divine*, 12–13.
14. *L'erede delle cose divine*, 12–13.
15. *L'erede delle cose divine*, 13.
16. *L'erede delle cose divine*, 14.
17. *L'erede delle cose divine*, 15.
18. *L'erede delle cose divine*, 15.
19. See Ps. 17, 6; 102, 2.
20. See Ps., 116, 2.
21. *L'erede delle cose divine*, 249.
22. *L'erede delle cose divine*, 259.
23. *L'erede delle cose divine*, 266.
24. Ps. 150, 3–5.
25. *En.*, 150, 6.
26. See *En.*, 150, 7.
27. Hilary of Poitiers, *Tractatus super Psalmos*, 150, 2.
28. See 1 Cor 15, 51.
29. Cf. Hilary of Poitiers, *Tractatus super Psalmos*, 150, 2: 'Thus we praise with well-tuned cymbals. This type of praise is perfected with the cymbals of exultation. Here is all the praise that you will find with the saints. The corruption of the flesh and of the blood will be far from them, and they will be reformed in the image of their Creator, beginning by then also to be conformed to the glory of the body of God.'
30. *En.*, 150, 7.
31. *En.*, 150, 7.
32. See 1 Cor 15, 41.

33 *En.*, 150, 5.
34 *En.*, 150, 8.
35 *En.*, 150, 8.
36 *En.*, 150, 8.
37 1 Cor 13, 13.
38 *En.*, 150, 8.
39 See *En.*, 150, 8.
40 Cf. Gen 2, 7; Is 57, 16.
41 Ps. 150, 1.
42 *En.*, 150, 8.
43 Cf., for example, *Serm.*, 34, 6.
44 *En.*, 150, 8.

Chapter 3

1 Cf. *Confess.*, XI, 7, 9.
2 Cf. Mark 9, 7; Matt. 17, 5; Luke 9, 35.
3 Cf. *Conf.*, XIII, 29, 44.
4 Cf. *De civ. Dei*, X, XV.
5 1 John 1, 1.
6 *En.*, 8, 2.
7 Cf. *De civ. Dei*, X, XIII.
8 *En.*, 8, 2. See also *De mus.*, I, 1, 1.
9 *Serm.*, 52, 16.
10 *En.*, 8, 8.
11 *En.*, 8, 2.
12 John 1, 23.
13 *Serm.*, 293, 3.
14 *En.*, 39, 15.
15 *Serm.*, 293, 3.
16 *In Io. Ev.*, I, 8.
17 *In Io. Ev.*, I, 8.
18 Guglielmo di Saint-Thierry, *Expositio super Cantica Canticorum*, 45.
19 See Mark, 9, 7; Matt. 17, 5; Luke 9, 35.
20 Mark 1, 11. See also Mark 9, 7; Luke 3, 22; Matt. 3, 17; Matt. 17, 5.
21 *c. s. Ar.*, 13, 9.
22 *De Trin.*, IV, 2, 4.
23 Cf. also Augustine, *De mus.*, I, V.
24 *De mus.*, IV, 3, 5–6; 4, 7; 6, 10.

25 *De mus.*, IV, 3, 6.
26 *De mus.*, IV, 3, 5.
27 See *En.*, 87, 1: 'Pro choro ad respondendum; nisi forte ut canenti chorus consonando respondeat?'
28 *En.*, 87, 1.
29 *En.*, 87, 1.
30 See *En.*, 87, 1: 'But the choir signifies concord, which consists in charity: whoever therefore in imitation of our Lord's Passion gives up his body to be burnt, if he have not charity, does not answer in the choir, and therefore it profits him nothing.'
31 *En.*, 87, 1.
32 *En.*, 87, 1.
33 *En.*, 87, 3.
34 Mark 14, 34.
35 See *En.*, 87, 3.
36 *En.*, 87, 3.
37 *En.*, 30 II disc. 1, 3.
38 *En.*, 30 II disc. 1, 3.
39 Mark 15, 34; Matt. 27, 46.
40 See *En.*, 37, 27. Cf. also *En.*, 41, 17.
41 *En.*, 49, 5.
42 *En.*, 43, 2.
43 *En.*, 40, 6.
44 *En.*, 40, 6.
45 Cf. *En.*, 29 II, 12.
46 Cf. *En.*, 29 II, 16.
47 Cf. *En.*, 56, 5.
48 *En.*, 34 II, 5.
49 *En.*, 34 II, 5.
50 *En.*, 34 II, 5.
51 See Luke 11, 9; Matt. 7, 7.
52 [*sine affect, sine misericordia* (Rom 1, 31)]. 'Ubi est affectus, ibi misericordia.'
53 *En.*, 33 II, 2.
54 *En.*, 33 II, 2.
55 *En.*, 33 II, 2: 'Tympanizabat autem ad ostia civitatis: quae sunt ostia civitatis, nisi corda nostra quae clauseramus contra Christum, qui de tympano crucis aperuit corda mortalium?'
56 See Matt. 27, 40: 'Come down from the cross, if you are the Son of God!'
57 *En.*, 33 I, 9.
58 *En.*, 33 I, 9.
59 See Bonaventura, *Vitis mystica*, VII, XIII.

60 *En.*, 32 I, 2; Rom 12, 1.
61 *En.*, 32 II, 22.
62 Cf. *Conf.*, X, 3, 3–4.
63 *En.*, 9, 33.
64 *En.*, 9, 33.
65 See *En.*, 30 II disc. 1, 7.
66 *En.*, 30 II disc. 1, 7.
67 *En.*, 30 II disc. 1, 7.
68 *De vera rel.*, 49, 94.
69 *En.*, 30 II disc. 1, 7.
70 *En.*, 30 II disc. 1, 7.
71 Cf. *En.*, 3, 4.
72 Cf. *En.*, 5, 2–3.
73 Cf. *En.*, 37, 13–14; *Conf.*, X, 3, 3–4.
74 Cf. *En.*, 76, 5–6.
75 *En.*, 5, 2.
76 *Conf.*, X, 3, 3–4.
77 *En.*, 31 I, 9.
78 *En.*, 29 I, 9.
79 *En.*, 29, I, 13.
80 See *En.*, 56, 16.
81 See *En.*, 56, 16.
82 *En.*, 56, 16.
83 *En.*, 56, 16.
84 *En.*, 56, 16.
85 *En.*, 56, 16.
86 *En.*, 56, 16.
87 *En.*, 56, 16.
88 *En.*, 7, 1.
89 See *En.*, 7, 1 (quoting Rom. 11, 33–4): 'O altitudo divitiarum sapientiae et scientiae Dei, quam inscrutabilia sunt iudicia eius, et investigabiles viae ipsius! Quis enim cognovit mentem Domini, aut quis consiliarius illius fuit?'
90 *En.*, 35, 17.
91 *En.*, 35, 17.
92 *En.*, 37, 20.
93 *En.*, 37, 20.
94 Cf. *De natura boni*, 15.
95 *De mus.*, VI, 13, 38.
96 1 John 2, 9–10.
97 *En.*, 7, 1.
98 *En.*, 7, 1.
99 *En.*, 7, 1.

100 *En.*, 21 II, 2.
101 *En.*, 21 II, 2.
102 Acts, 4, 20.
103 See Ps. 92, 3.
104 *En.*, 92, 7.
105 *En.*, 38, 5.
106 Cf. Ps. 38, 10.
107 See *En.*, 38, 4.
108 Ps. 136, 1–3.
109 Cf. *En.*, 136, 1–2.
110 *En.*, 86, 1; see also 1 Cor. 2, 9.
111 *En.*, 86, 1.
112 *En.*, 86, 1.
113 See *En.*, 136, 6.
114 See Rev. 18, 22.
115 See *En.*, 136, 6.
116 See *En.*, 136, 6.
117 See *En.*, 136, 6.
118 See *En.*, 136, 6.
119 See *En.*, 136, 6: 'Non ergo eis organa nostra inserendo alligamus, sed differendo suspendimus.'
120 John 16, 12.
121 See *En.*, 136, 10.
122 *En.*, 136, 10.
123 *En.*, 136, 10.
124 *En.*, 136, 10.
125 *En.*, 136, 10.
126 *En.*, 136, 10.
127 *En.*, 136, 13.
128 See Matt. 19, 16.
129 *En.*, 136, 13.
130 *En.*, 136, 13.
131 Ps. 136, 4.
132 *En.*, 136, 13; Ps. 136, 4.
133 See Tim 6, 17.
134 *En.*, 136, 13.
135 Cf. *En.*, 136, 13.
136 *En.*, 136, 13.
137 *En.*, 136, 15.
138 *En.*, 136, 22.
139 Ps. 136, 6.
140 *En.*, 136, 17.

Chapter 4

1 *En.*, 44, 29.
2 2 Cor. 12, 4.
3 Cf., for example, *En.*, 39, 6.
4 Cf. *En.*, 34 II, 6.
5 Cf. *En.*, 30 II disc. 1, 2.
6 See Rev. 5, 9; 14, 3.
7 *En.*, 32 II disc. 1, 8.
8 *En.*, 143, 16.
9 *En.*, 143, 16.
10 *En.*, 32 II disc. 1, 8.
11 *En.*, 32 II disc. 1, 8.
12 *En.*, 32 II disc. 1, 8.
13 Cf., for example, *De mus.*, I, 5, 10; II, 2, 2; II, 12, 21–3; III, 8, 18: IV, 16, 30; IV, 11, 12; VI, 2, 3.
14 Cf. *En.*, 4, 1.
15 *En.*, 32 II disc. 1, 8.
16 *En.*, 32 II disc. 1, 8.
17 Ps. 94, 9.
18 See Rev. 15, 3.
19 *En.*, 32 II disc. 1, 8.
20 *En.*, 32 II disc. 1, 8: 'Quid est in iubilatione canere? Intellegere, verbis explicare non posse quod canitur corde.'
21 *De Mag.*, 1, 2. Cf. also *En.*, 37, 28; Matt. 6, 5–7.
22 *En.*, 32 II disc. 1, 8.
23 *En.*, 99, 4.
24 *De Trin.*, IV, 2, 4.
25 Cf. Aristotle, *L'anima*, II, 8, 420*a-b*.
26 *En.*, 32 II disc. 1, 8.
27 *En.*, 32 II disc. 2, 2.
28 *De Magistro*, 1, 1.
29 *De Magistro*, 1, 1.
30 *De Magistro*, 7, 19.
31 Ps. 47, 5.
32 *En.*, 46, 7.
33 See, for example, Lev. 23, 24; 25, 9; 1 Sam 13, 3; 2 Sam 2, 28; 15, 10; 1 Kings 1, 34; Ps. 46, 6; Rev. 8, 7.
34 Ps. 47, 6.
35 See *En.*, 46, 9.
36 *En.*, 46, 9.
37 *En.*, 46, 9.
38 *En.*, 3, 4.

39 *En.*, 33 II, 8; Cf. Matt. 6, 6.
40 *En.*, 33 II, 8.
41 *En.*, 26 I, 8. See Ps. 26, 8.
42 See *En.*, 3, 10.
43 See *En.*, 76, 11–12.
44 See *En.*, 46, 9.
45 See *En.*, 109, 7.
46 Cf. *De mus.*, VI, 11, 33.
47 Cf. Eccl. 5, 1.
48 Mark 2, 6; 2, 8.
49 See 1 Rom 3, 9; 5, 9; Prov. 6, 32; 7, 7; Is 65, 17; Jer. 3, 16.
50 Eccl. 5, 1.
51 Mark 2, 8.
52 See *En.*, 40, 2.
53 *En.*, 64, 4.
54 *En.*, 42, 7.
55 *En.*, 41, 9.
56 *En.*, 41, 9.
57 Joshua 6, 20.
58 See *En.*, 41, 9.
59 *En.*, 41, 9.
60 *En.*, 41, 9.
61 *En.*, 41, 10.
62 See *En.*, 41, 10.
63 Ps. 42, 5.
64 *En.*, 41, 10.
65 *En.*, 37, 2.
66 *En.*, 41, 9.
67 *En.*, 41, 9.
68 See *En.*, 42, 7.
69 Cf. for example *En.*, 41, 9; 42, 7; *Conf.*, VIII, 10, 16.
70 See Matt. 6, 6.
71 Cf. *En.*, 41, 9.
72 See *De mus.*, V, 13, 28.
73 Cf. *De vera rel.*, 42, 79.
74 See John 3, 29.
75 Cf. *De mus.*, VI, 8.
76 Cf. for example *De mus.*, II, 13, 27; *De ord.*, II, 11, 33; *En.*, 41, 9; *Conf.*, X, 33, 50.
77 See *De mus.*, II, 13, 27.
78 Cf. *De vera rel.*, 42, 79.
79 See *De mus.*, I, 13, 28.
80 See *Conf.*, X, 33, 49.
81 See Jer. 17, 9.

BIBLIOGRAPHY

AMERIO, FRANCO
1929 *Il De musica di sant'Agostino*, Torino, Società editrice internazionale.

BEIERWALTES, WERNER
1975 'Aequalitas numerosa. Zu Augustins Begriff des Schönen', *Wissenschaft und Weisheit*, 38, p. 140–57, traduzione Italiana, *Agostino e il Neoplatonismo cristiano*, Vita e pensiero, Milano, 1995, p. 159–86.

BETTETINI, MARIAS
1992 *Ordine, musica, bellezza*, Milano, Rusconi.
1994 *La misura delle cose. Struttura e modelli dell'universo secondo Agostino d'Ippona*, Milano, Rusconi.
1997 *Musica*, testo latino a fronte, Milano, Rusconi.
1999 'Al limiti della materia, tra neoplatonismo e cristianesimo. Per una lettura del "De musica" di Agostino d'Ippona', T. Fuhrer, M. Erler and K. Schlapbach (eds.), *Zur Rezeption der hellenistischen Philosophie in der Spätantike*, Franz Steiner Verlag, Stuttgart, p. 123–38.
2001 'Musica tra cielo e terra: lettura del De musica di Agostino d'Ippona', Mauro Letterio, *La musica nel pensiero medievale*, Ravenna, Longo, p. 103–22.

BOCCADORO, BRENNO
2019 'Remarques sur les essais sur l'origine de la musique où il est parlé d'ornithonlogie', *Poésie*, 167-8, 1–2, p. 89–111.

BOWEN, WILLIAM R.
1988 'St. Augustine in Medieval and Renaissance Musical Science', R. R. La Croix (ed.), *Augustine on Music. An Interdisciplinary Collection of Essays*, New York, Edwin Mellen Press, p. 29–51.

BRENNAN, BRIAN
1988 'Augustine's "De musica"', *Vigiliae Christianae*, 42, p. 267–81.

BROWN, HOWARD MAYER
1984 'St. Augustine, Lady Music, and the Gittern in Fourteenth-Century Italy', *Musica Disciplina*, 38, p. 25–65.

CANETTIERI, PAOLO
1998 'La metrica e la "numerabilità" del tempo', *Il testo e il tempo. Critica del testo*, I, 1, p. 141–76.

CATAPANO, GIOVANNI (ed.)
2006 *Agostino. Tutti i dialoghi*, testo latino a fronte, Milano, Bompiani.
CHARRU, PHILIPPE
2009 'Temps et musique dans la pensée d'Augustin', *Revue d'études augustiniennes et patristiques*, 55, p. 171–88.
CORBIN, SOLANGE
1962 '"Musica" spéculative et "cantus" pratique. Le rôle de saint Augustin dans la transmission des sciences musicales', *Cahiers de civilisation médiévale*, 5, p. 1–12.
1983 *La musica cristiana dalla origini al gregoriano*, Milano, Jaca Book (traduzione italiana di: *L'Eglise à la conquête de sa musique*, Paris, Gallimard,1963).
COSTA, DANIELA
1989–1990 *Il pensiero di sant'Agostino sulla musica*, Tesi di laurea dell'Università degli Studi di Torino.
1993 'Sant'Agostino e le allegorie degli strumenti musicali', *Répertoire International d'Iconographie Musicale*, 28, p. 207–26.
COURT, RAYMOND
1987 *Sagesse de l'art*, Paris, Méridiens Klincksieck.
CROCKER, RICHARD L.
1958 'Musica Rhythmica and Musica Metrica in Antique and Medieval Theory', *Journal of Music Theory*, 2, p. 2–23.
CROCKER, RICHARD and HILEY, DAVID (eds.),
1990 *New Oxford History of Music*, vol. 2, 'The Early Middle Ages to 1300', Oxford, New York, Oxford University Press.
CROSSLEY, GOULBURN W.
1951 'St. Augustine's "De musica": A Recent Synopsis', *The Musical Times*, 92, p. 127–9.
DE CROZALS, J.
1894 'Quelques théories de s. Augustin sur la métrique d'après son traité de la musique', *Ann. enseign. sup. Grenoble*, 4, p. 499–540.
DEHNERT, EDMUND J.
1969 'Music as Liberal in Augustine and Boethius', *Arts libéraux et Philosophie au Moyen Age. Actes du Quatrième Congrés international de philosophie médiévale, Université de Montréal, Canada, 24 aôut - 2 septembre 1967*, Montréal,Institut d'Etudes Médiévales, p. 987–91.
DUSSÀN, MAXIMILIANO P.
2003 'Lectura de los diálogos "De ordine" y "De musica" de San Agustín, a partir de la idea de ascenso del hombre hacia Dios a través de la música', *Franciscanum*, 45, p. 65–153.
DYER, JOSEPH
1981 'Augustin and the "Hymni ante oblationem". The Earliest Offertory Chants?' *Revue des études augustiniennes*, 27, p. 85–99.

EICHHORN, ANDREAS
1996 'Augustinus und die Musik', *Musica*, 50, p. 318–23.

ELDELSTEIN, HEINZ
1929 *Die Musikanschauung Augustins nach seiner Schrift 'De musica'*, Ohlan.

ENGLAND, F.
2017 'Music, Theology and Space. Listening as a Way of Seeking God', *Acta Theologica*, 37, 1, p. 18–40.

EVERIST, MARK (ed.),
2011 *The Cambridge Companion to Medieval Music*, Cambridge, Cambridge University Press.

FEDRIGA, RICCARDO
2012 'Per voce sola. Lo *Iubilus* e il canto senza parola', V. Minazzi e C. Ruini (ed.), *Atlante storico della musica nel Medioevo*, Milano, Jaca Book, p. 30–1.

FOGLEMAN, ALEX
2019 'Becoming the Song of Christ. Musical Theology and Transformation Grace in Augustine's Enarratio in Psalmum 32', *Augustinian Studies* 50, 2, p. 133–50.

FOLLI, LAURA
2001 '"Canticum cordis": la musica e l'interiorità nelle Enarrationes in Psalmos di Agostino', in Mauro Letterio, *La musica nel pensiero medievale*, Ravenna, Longo, p. 177–84.

FÖLLMI, BEAT
1994 *Das Weiterwirken der Musikanschauung Augustins im 16. Jahrhundert*, Bern, Peter Lang (Europäische Hochschulschriften, XXXVI/116).

FORMAN, ROBERT J.
1988 'Augustine's Music: "Keys" to the Logos', R. R. La Croix (ed.), *Augustine on Music. An Interdisciplinary Collection of Essays Augustine on Music*, New York, Edwin Mellen Press, p. 17–27.

FRITZ, JEAN-MARIE
2018 'Cithares à géométrie variable dans les exégèses médiévales des Psaumes ou Comment la pensée sérielle crée l'instrument de musique', in *La pensée sérielle, du Moyen Age aux Lumières*, Cahiers de recherche des Instituts néerlandais de langue et de littérature française, 65, Leiden, Brill, p. 108–28.

FROVA, CARLA
1985 'La musica nell'insegnamento delle arti liberali : i trattati di S. Agostino e Boezio', *Benedictina*, 2, 32, p. 377–88.

FUBINI, ENRICO
1976 *L'estetica musicale dall'antichità al Settecento*, Einaudi, Torino.

GAMBER, KLAUS
1969 'Ordo Missae Africanae. Der nord-afr. Messritus zur Zeit des hl. Augustinus', *Röm. Quartalschrift für christl. Altertumskunde und Kirchengesch.* 64, p. 139–53.

GEROLD, THÉODORE
1931 *Les Pères de l'Eglise et la musique*, Strasbourg, Imprimerie Alsacienne.

GOLDMAN, DAVID
1985 'Augustinus und die Mögligkeit einer musikalischen Renaissance', *Der Hl. Augustinus, Vater der europäisch-afrikanischen Zivilisation. 5. internationale Konferenz des Schiller-Instituts, 1.-3. November 1985 in Rom*, Wiesbaden, Dr. Böttiger Verlags, p. 175–88.

GONZALÉS, PALOMA O.
2005 *El De musica de san Agustín y la tradición pitagórico-platónica*, Valladolid, Estudio agustiniano.

GUANTI, GIOVANNI
1987 'La musica come metafora teologica in Agostino e in Kierkegaard', *Rivista di Estetica*, 27, p. 153–69.
1990 'Tempo musicale e tempo storico in Agostino e in Kierkegaard', *Revue Esthétique*, 30, p. 95–141.

HARRISON, CAROL
2011 'Augustine and the Art of Music', J. S. Begbie and S. R. Guthrie (eds.), *Resonant Witness: Conversations between Music and Theology*, Eerdmans, Calvin Institute of Christian Worship Liturgical Studies, p. 27–45.
2015 'Getting Carried Away: Why Did Augustine Sing?' *Augustinian Studies* 46, 1, p. 1–22.
2019 *On Music, Sense, Affect and Voice*, New York, Bloomsbury, Reading Augustine.

HENTSCHEL, FRANK
1994 'Sinnlichkeit und Vernunft in Augustins "De musica"', *Wissenschaft und Weisheit*, 57, p. 189–200.
2002 *De musica: Bücher I und VI: Vom ästhetischen Urteil zur metaphysischen Erkenntnis*, Hamburg, Meiner, Philosophische Bibliothek, 539.

HOFFMANN, WILHELM
1931 *Philosophische Interpretation der Augustinusschrift de arte musica*, PhD dissertation, Freiburg, University of Freiburg.

HONORATO, MARIA del PILAR MONTERO
1988 'La mùsica en san Agustìn', *Studium Ovetense*, XVI, p. 153–96.

HORN, CHRISTOPH
1994 'Augustins Philosophie der Zahlen', *Revue des études augustiniennes*, 40, p. 389–415.

JORDAN, WILLIAM
1990 'Augustine on Music', MEYNELL (ed.), *Grace, Politics and Desire: Essays on Augustine*, Calgary, Alberta, The University of Calgary, p. 123-35.

JUAREZ, AGUSTÌN U.
1998 'San Augstín. Belleza, música e istoria. "Un admirable cántico"', *Augustinus*, 169, p. 107-28.

KIM HYE YOUNG
2019 'Melody, Rhythm, Time: Phenomenology of Music in Augustine, Brentano and Husserl', *Glimpse*, 18, p. 61-9.

KNIGHT, JACKSON W. F.
1949 *St. Augustine's 'De musica': A Synopsis*, London, Orthological Institute.

KOLLER, H.
1981 'Die Silbenquantitäten in Augustinus's Büchen *De musica*', *Museum Helveticum*, 38, p. 262-7.

LE BOEUF, PATRICK
1986 'La tradition manuscrite du *De musica* de saint Augustin et son influence sur la pensée et l'esthétique médiévale', *Positions de thèses*, Paris, Ecole des Chartes, p. 107-15.
1987 'Un commentaire d'inspiration érigénienne du *De musica* de saint Augustin', *Recherches Augustiniennes*, 22, p. 243-316.

LEMOS, Fernando A.
2001 '"Proportio habens medium duoque extrema". A média aritmética e média harmónica nas "Confissões", de Santo Agostinho', *Actas do congresso internacional, as Confissões de Santo Agostinho*, Lisboa, Universidade Católica Editora, p. 671-96.

MAHRT, WILLIAM P.
2018 'St. Augustine's Time and Eternity in Medieval Music', *Sacred Music*, 145, 4, p. 6-14.

MARROU, HENRI-IRÉNÉE
1938 *Saint Augustin et la fin de la culture antique*, Paris, De Boccard.
1939 'Tristesse de l'historien', *Esprit* traduzione di Giulio Colombi, *Tristezza dello storico. Possibilità e limiti della storiografia* a cura di Maurilio Guasco, Brescia, Morcelliana, 1999.
1942 *Traité de musique selon l'esprit de saint Augustin*, Paris, Le Seuil; *Il silenzio e la storia. Trattato della musica secondo lo spirito di sant'Agostino*, Milano, Edizioni Medusa, 2007 traduzione di Riccardo Campi con una prefazione di Marzio Pieri e nota introduttiva di Pier Angelo Carozzi.

MASSIN, MARIANNA
2011 'La musique selon saint Augustin, une rédemption du sensible?' F. Malhomme et E. Villari (ed.), *Muisca corporis. Savoirs et arts du*

corps de l'Antiquité à l'âge umaniste et classique, Turnhout, Brepols, p. 139–58.

MATTEUCCI, GIUSEPPE
1985 '"De musica" des Hl. Augustinus: Musik als Wissenschaft des Geistes', *Der Hl. Augustinus, Vater der europäisch-afrikanischen Zivilisation. 5. internationale Konferenz des Schiller-Instituts, 1.-3. November 1985 in Rom*, Wiesbaden, Dr. Böttiger Verlags, p. 170–4.

MCKINNON, JAMES W.
1968 'Musical Instruments in Medieval Psalm Commentaries and Psalters', *Journal of the American Musicological Society*, 21, p. 3–20.

MEYER-BAER, KATHI
1953 'Psychologic and Ontologic Ideas in Augustine's *De musica*', *The Journal of Aesthetics and Art Criticism*, 11, p. 224–30.

MEYNELL, HUGO (ed.)
1990 *Grace, Politics and Desire: Essays on Augustine*, Calgary, Alberta, The University of Calgary, p. 123–35.

MICHEL, ALAIN
1990 'Sagesse et spiritualité dans la parole et dans la musique: de Cicéron à saint Augustin', M. von Albrecht and W. Schubert (eds.), *Musik und Dichtung: neue Forschungsbeiträge, Viktor Pöschl zum 80. Geburtstag gewidmet*, Frankfurt, Lang, p. 133–44.

MICHELET, MARCEL
1943 'De la musique au silence. Notes sur l'usage de la joie esthétique d'après Saint Augustin', *Revue des Etudes Latines*, 21–2, p. 30–2.

MICUNCO, GIUSEPPE
2007 *Canta chi ama. La musica e il canto in sant'Agostino*, Bari, Stilo Editrice.

MONETA CAGLIO, ERNESTO T.
1976–1977 'Lo *Iubilus* e le origini della Salmodia Responsoriale', *Jucunda Laudatio*, 15, p. 5–17.

MORAO, ARTUR
2001 'A musica como realidade e como metafora, nas "Confissões"', *Actas do congresso internacional, as Confissões de Santo Agustinho*, Lisboa, Universidade Católica Editora, p. 729–44.

NOWAK, ADOLF
1975 'Die *numeri judiciales* des Augustinus und ihre musik-theoritische Bedeutung', *Archiv für Musikforschung*, XXXII, 3, p. 196–207.

PABÓN, GUILLERMO L.C.
2011 *Numerus-proportio en el De Musica de San Agustín: La tradición pitagórico-platónica*, Editorial Académica Española.

PANTI, CECILIA
2007 '*Verbum cordis e ministerium vocis*. Il canto emozionale di Agostino e le visioni sonore di Ildegarda di Bingen', in M. Cristiani, C. Panti and

G. Perillo (eds.), *Armonia mundi. Musica Mondana e Musica Celeste fra Antichità e Medioevo*, Firenze, Edizioni del Galluzzo, p. 155–87.
2008 *Filosofia della musica. Tarda Antichità e Medioevo*, Roma, Carocci.
2010 'Il suono che tace. Silenzio e pausa in Sant'Agostino e nella teoria musicale medievale', *Micrologus*, 18, p. 3–28.

PAREDI, ANGELO
1988 'Le innovazioni musicali di Sant'Ambrogio nei commenti di Sant'Agostino', *Rivista internazionale di musica sacra*, 9, p. 211–14.

PARODI, MASSIMO
2011 'Agostino. La musica, i numeri e la relazione', V. Minazzi e C. Ruini (ed.), *Atlante storico della musica nel Medioevo*, Milano, Jaca Book, p. 40–5.

PERL, CARL J.
1937 'Musik und Geist. Die mus. Schriften des hl. Augustinus', *Musica sacra*, 65, p. 97–100.
1954 'Augustinus und die Musik', *Schweizer. Musikzrg.*, 94, p. 402–41.

PERL, CARL J. and KRIEGSMAN, A.
1955 'Augustine and Music: On the Occasion of the 1600th Anniversary of the Saint', *The Musical Quarterly*, 41, p. 496–550.

PHILLIPS, NANCY and HUGLO, MICHEL
1985 'Le "De musica" de saint Augustin et l'organisation de la durée musicale du IXe au XIIe siècles', *Recherches Augustiniennes*, 20, p. 117–31.

PICKSTOCK, CATHERINE
1998 'Ascending Numbers: Augustine's "De musica" and the Western Tradition', L. O. Ayres and G. Jones (eds.), *Christian Origins.Theology, Rhetoric and Community*, London-New York, Routledge, p. 185–215.
1999 'Music: Soul, City and Cosmos after Augustine', J. Milbank, C. Pickstock and G. Ward (eds.), *Radical Orthodoxy: A New Theology*, London-New York, Routledge, p. 243–77.

PIQUÉ-COLLADO, JORGE A.
2006 *Teología y música: Una contribución dialécto-trascendental sobre la sacramentalidad de la percepción estética del Misterio (Augustín, Balthasar, Sequeri; Victoria, Schönberg, Messiaen)*, Roma, Pontificia Università Gregoriana.

PIZZANI, UBALDO
1978 'Spunti escatologici nel *De musica* di S. Agostino', *Augustinianum*, 18, p. 209–18.
1990 'Intentio ed escatologia nel sesto libro del *De musica* di S. Agostino', L. Alici (ed.), *Interiorità e Intenzionalità in S. Agostino. Atti del I° e II° Seminario Internazionale del Centro di Studi Agostiniani di Perugia*, Roma, Instututum Patrisitcum Augustinianum, p. 35–57.

1994 'La "musica disciplina" tra Agostino e Boezio', A. Privitera (ed.), *Paideia cristiana. Studi in onore di Mario Naldini*, Roma, Gruppo Editoriale Internazionela, p. 347–64.

2000 'L'eredità di Agostino e la cultura classica', *Sentimento del tempo e periodizzazione della storia nel Medioevo. Atti del XXXVI Convegno storico internazionale, Todi, 10-12 ottobre 1999*, Spoleto, Centro Italiano di Studi sull'Alto Medioevo, p. 47–67.

2003a 'Du rapport entre le *De musica* de S. Augustin et le *De institutione musica* de Boèce', A. Galonnier (ed.), *Boèce ou la chaîne des savoirs. Actes du colloque international de la fondation Singer-Polignac, Paris 8-12 juin 1999*, Louvain-la-Neuve, Paris, Editions de l'Institut supérieur de philosophie-Editions Peteers, p. 357–77.

2003b 'S. Agostino e la musica alla luce delle "Confessioni"', *Le 'Confessioni di Agostino (402-2002). Bilancio e prospettive, XXXI Incontro di studiosi dell'antichità cristiana, Roma, 2-4 maggio 2002*, Roma, Institutum Patrisitcum Augustinianum, p. 487–98.

PROIETTI, PIERLUCA

1999 'Numero e musica nel medioevo: Da Agostino alla complessità del Quattrocento', L. Mauro (ed.), *La musica nel pensiero medievale*, Ravenna, Longo, p. 71–80.

PUGLIATTI, SALVATORE

1947 'S. Agostino e l'estetica musicale dei Greci', *Teoremi*, 2, p. 182–99.

REY ALTUNA, LUIS

1960 'San Agustín y la música', *Augustinus*, 5, p. 191–206.

SALLMANN, KLAUS

1990 'Augustinus' Rettung der Musik und die antike Mimesistheorie', H. Eisenberger (ed.), *Epmheymata. Festschrift für Hadwig Hörner zum sechzigsten Geburtstag*, Heidelberg, Carl Winter-Universitätsverlag, p. 81–92.

SCHERER, W.

1909 'Uber die VI Bücher *De musica*', *Kirchenmusikalischen Jahrbuch*, 22, p. 62–9.

SCHMITT, ARBOGAST

1990 'Zahl und Schönheit in Augustine "De musica, VI"', *Würzburger Jahrbücher für die Altertumswiss*, 16, p. 221–37.

SCHNEIDER, A.

1939 'Aurelius Augustinus und die Musik', *Benediktinische Monatsschrift*, 21, p. 210–12.

SIERRA, JOSÉ

1986 'Agustin, enamorado de la musica', *La Escuela Agustiniana*, 24, p. 131–6.

SKERIS, R.
1984–1985 'Via nova, viator novus, canticum novum. The Theology of Praise in Song According to Augustine's *Discours on the Psalms*', *Musices aptatio*, p. 69–100.

STEFANI, GINO
1969 *L'Etica musicale di S. Agostino*, Roma, Pontificia Università Lateranensis.

VAGAGGINI, CIPRIANO
1964 'La teologia della lode secondo S. Agostino', *La preghiera nella Bibbia e nella tradizione patristica e monastica*, C. Vagaggini e G. Penco (ed.), Roma, Edizioni Paoline, p. 399–467.

VAN WYMEERSCH, BRIGITTE
2002 'Saint Augustin: nombre et beauté', Lenain, D. Lories (ed.), *Esthétique et philosophie de l'art. Repères historiques et thématiques*, Bruxelles, De Boeck, p 41–6.

VECCHI, GIUSEPPE
1951 'Praecepta artis musicae collecta ex libris sex Aurelii Augustini De musica', *Memorie della Reale Accademia delle scienze dell'istituto di Bologna*, Classe di scienze morali, Ser. 5, 1, 1950, Bologna, Accademia delle scienze dell'Istituto di Bologna, p. 91–153.

VENDRIX, PHILIPPE
1992 'L'Augustinisme musical en France au XVIIe siècle', *Revue de Musicologie*, 78, p. 237–55.

VERHEUL, AMBROISE
1983 'La spiritualité du chant liturgique chez saint Paul et saint Augustin', *Questions liturgiques*, 64, p. 165–78.

VON ALBRECHT, MICHEAL
1993 'Zu Augustinus Musikverständnis in den "Confessiones"', G. W. Most (ed.), *Philanthropia kai Eusebeia. Festschrift für Albrecht Dihle zum 70. Geburtstag*, Göttingen, Vandenhoeck & Ruprecht, p. 1–16.

WALHOUT, DONALD
1989 'Augustine on the Transcendent in Music', *Philosophy and Theology*, 3, p. 283–93.

WISKUS, JESSICA
2016 'Rhythm and Transformation through Memory. On Augustine's Confessions after De Musica', *The Journal of Speculative Philosophy*, 30, 3, p. 328–38.

WUIDAR, LAURENCE
2009 '*Confessioni* e speculazioni musicali: l'immagine sonora nell'opera agostiniana', *Divus Thomas, Commentarium de Philosophia et Theologia*, 112, 2, p. 133–63.
2010 'Parola segreta e trasporto gioioso: la metafora musicale nel commento agostiniano al salmo 32 e nel *De venatione sapientiae* di Cusano', *Divus Thomas, Commentarium de Philosophia et Theologia*, 113, 3, p. 66–84.

2011 'Oltre le parole: suono, silenzio, sguardo, gesto. Teorie agostiniane e bernardiane del linguaggio affettivo', *Divus Thomas, Commentarium de Philosophia et Theologia*, 114, 3, p. 114–32.
2015a 'L'immagine musicale quale riflesso dell'eternità. Note agostiniane', a cura di Paolo Gozza, *L'immagine musicale*, Milano, Mimesis, p. 25–43.
2015b 'Iconologie de la voix: du sermon de voce e verbo au Traitez de la voix et des chants', *Matèria. Revista internacional d'Art*, 9, p. 15–38.
2016a 'Voix visible et musique intelligible chez Philon d'Alexandrie', *Divus Thomas, Commentarium de Philosophia et Theologia*, 119, 1, p. 159–79.
2016b *L'uomo musicale nell'antico cristianesimo. Storia di una metafora tra Oriente e Occidente*, Bruxelles – Roma, Institut Historique Belge de Rome.
2017a 'La metafora musicale dal De mysteriis all'Incendium amoris: possessione divina, alienazione musicale e trasporto mistico', a cura di Francesco Finocchiaro – Maurizio Giani, *Musica e metafora: storia analisi ermeneutica*, Biblioteca di Athena Musica, Torino, Academia University Press, p. 3–22.
2017b 'La musique dans l'In inscriptiones Psalmorum de Grégoire de Nysse', *Revue belge de musicologie*, 7, p. 5–32.
2019 "Ineffability and music in early Christian theology ", in Robert A. Yelle – Christopher I. Lehrich – Courtney Handman (éds.), Language and Religion, Berlin-Boston, De Gruyter, p. 215–42.
2019 "Introduction", in Laurence Wuidar – René Wetzel (eds.), *Mystique, langage, musique. Exprimer l'indicible au Moyen âge*, Scrinium Friburgense, Wiesbaden, Reichert Verlag, p. VII–XVIII.
2019 "Le langage musical face à l'indicible", in Laurence Wuidar – René Wetzel (Eds.), *Mystique, langage, musique. Exprimer l'indicible au Moyen âge*, Scrinium Friburgense, Wiesbaden, Reichert Verlag, p. 15–34.
2021 *Fuga Divina. La musique dans l'écrit mystique du Moyen âge à la première modernité*, Genève, Droz, Cahiers d'Humanisme et Renaissance, p. 173.
2021 'Secret song and visionary music in Hadewich d'Anvers', Claire Fontijn (éd.), *Uncovering the Music of Early European Women*, London, Routledge.

ZORZI, BENEDETTA M.
2002a 'L'esperienza del canto liturgico secondo le *Enarrationes in Psalmos* di Sant'Agostino', *Inter Fratres*, 52, 1, p. 27–52; 52/2, p. 211–38.
2002b 'Melos e Iubilus nelle Enarrationes in Psalmos di Agostino. Una questione di mistica agostiniana', *Augustinianum*, 42, p. 383–413.
2007 'Cuori con-cordi ma non all'uni-sono. L'allegoria alla vita cristiana della *vox strumentalis* nelle *Enarrationes in Psalmos* di S. Agostino', *Reportata. Passato e presente della teologia* [rivista in linea], http://mondodomani.org/reportata/zorzi07.htm.

INDEX

Confessiones xv, xvi, xviii, xix, 3, 4, 8, 12, 14, 28, 40, 77, 93, 94, 96, 125, 127
C.s. Ar. 82

De civitate Dei 77, 78
De mag. 112, 114
De musica xvi, xvii, xviii, xix, 12, 13, 45, 55, 56, 78, 84, 111, 117, 125-7
De nat. Boni 100
De ordine 12, 21
De Trinitate xvi, 2, 3, 83, 114
De vera religione xvi, xvii, xviii, 4, 12, 93, 125

Epistolae 15, 18, 20, 21, 43
Enarrationes in psalmos
En. in ps. 3 : 93, 116
En. in ps. 4 : 111
En. in ps. 5 : 94, 96
En. in ps. 6 : 22
En. in ps. 7 : 99–101
En. in ps. 8 : 78, 79
En. in ps. 9 : 93
En. in ps. 12 : 26, 46
En. in ps. 17 : 46
En. in ps. 19 : 65
En. in ps. 21 : 101
En. in ps. 25 : 34
En. in ps. 26 : 43–5, 67, & 16
En. in ps. 29 : 88, 96
En. in ps. 30 : 28, 29, 88, 93, 110

En. in ps. 31 : 96
En. in ps. 32 : 47–9, 51, 57, 58, 71, 72, 74, 91, 92, 97, 110–14
En. in ps. 33 : 90–2, 116
En. in ps. 34 : 88, 89, 110
En. in ps. 35 : 45–6, 100
En. in ps. 36 : 46
En. in ps. 37 : 88, 94, 100, 103, 114, 123
En. in ps. 38 : 29, 33, 102
En. in ps. 39 : 28, 33, 44, 79, 110
En. in ps. 40 : 88, 118
En. in ps. 41 : 88, 121–5
En. in ps. 42 : 47–50, 52–4, 63, 71, 120, 124, 125
En. in ps. 43 : 88
En. in ps. 44 : 32, 109
En. in ps. 46 : 115–17
En. in ps. 47 : 22, 27
En. in ps. 48 : 31, 39–42
En. in ps. 49 : 32, 37, 38, 88
En. in ps. 50 : 40, 67
En. in ps. 53 : 38
En. in ps. 55 : 33
En. in ps. 56 : 88, 97, 98
En. in ps. 64 : 118
En. in ps. 71 : 34, 35
En. in ps. 72 : 36, 37
En. in ps. 76 : 35, 94, 117
En. in ps. 80 : 47, 59, 60, 71
En. in ps. 86 : 103
En. in ps. 87 : 85–7

En. in ps. 89 : 22, 55
En. in ps. 91 : 48, 60–2, 71
En. in ps. 92 : 31, 102
En. in ps. 99 : 113, 114
En. in ps. 109 : 65, 66, 117
En. in ps. 136 : 102–8

En. in ps. 143 : 61, 110
En. in ps. 150 : 22, 71, 73–6

In Io. Ev. 81

Sermones 44, 79, 80